Fifteen years ago, especially in Europe and the UK, the church planting movement was in its infancy. Today it is, we could say, in its early adolescence. Many things have been learned but new challenges lie ahead. Therefore, I am glad for the new edition of this book, in which those early lessons can be reviewed and the new horizons faced. I welcome this contribution to the literature of church planting in the 21st century.

TIM KELLER
Founding Pastor, Redeemer Presbyterian Church, New York City, New York

Multiplying churches through church planting movements involves warfare and wisdom. It is warfare because the evil one works for our defeat and destruction. It requires wisdom because we need to know how to engage the many battles we will face until Jesus returns. *Multiplying Churches* addresses well both of these and I delight in commending it to those willing to be on the front lines.

DANIEL L. AKIN
President, Southeastern Baptist Theological Seminary,
Wake Forest, North Carolina

Multiplying Churches provides a biblical foundation and theological parameters for church planting activities. Many church planting 'how-to' books and manuals exist. And while such resources are important, they often lack a thorough discussion of our Father's thoughts and desires about such missionary work. This book fills an important gap in the literature. Read it prayerfully with your Bible in hand, then make application to your life and ministry!

J. D. PAYNE
author, missiologist, and pastor of church multiplication,
The Church at Brook Hills, Birmingham, Alabama

Steve Timmis and friends have put together a short, readable book that is good for church planters, and all pastors. From the heights of biblical theology, to the plains of who does what, these brief chapters are again and again both practical and wise. I happily commend this book.

MARK DEVER
Pastor, Capitol Hill Baptist Church, Washington D.C.
President, 9Marks.org

Acts 29 has become a global leader in church planting, and I've benefited by learning from the leaders of the movement. Now you can learn from them as well. In *Multiplying Churches*, the au   vision for church planting that is gospel rich, but helpfu

Billy Graham Chair, Wheat

This is not another 'how to' book – nor is it simply about planting churches. The authors fully recognise the unique centrality of the church in God's purposes and therefore inevitably re-open fundamental questions concerning the nature of both the church and the gospel itself. Whether you are excited or disturbed by some of the answers given, it is always good to have traditional assumptions challenged from a solid biblical base. This volume is a valuable contribution to a vital debate. I hope its intention of stirring us to radical thinking and acting will be fully realised.'

JONATHAN STEPHEN
Provost and Lecturer in Preaching,
Union School of Theology, Bridgend, Wales

Church Planting must be the priority of all Christians. It is, in fact, just another word for evangelism and is the life-blood of the church. It is hard to imagine any strong and vibrant Gospel-centred group of people who are not concerned with spreading the Good News to another group of people and establishing a fellowship there. Steve Timmis has done us all a favour by bringing together these different contributions and various stories which illustrate to us not only the uniqueness of our message and the importance of the task but also the many different ways in which God works in people's lives. Read this book and be greatly encouraged.

FRANK RETIEF
Bishop, Church of England in South Africa

MULTIPLYING CHURCHES

EXPLORING GOD'S MISSION STRATEGY

EDITED BY STEVE TIMMIS

NEW & UPDATED EDITION

ACTS 29
churches planting churches

CHRISTIAN
FOCUS

Copyright © 2016

paperback ISBN 978-1-78191-324-6
epub ISBN 978-1-78191-958-3
mobi ISBN 978-1-78191-959-0

10 9 8 7 6 5 4 3 2 1

Published in 2016
by
Christian Focus Publications Ltd,
Geanies House, Fearn, Ross-shire,
IV20 1TW, Great Britain.

www.christianfocus.com

Cover design by Daniel van Straaten

Printed and bound
by
Bell & Bain, Glasgow

CONTENTS

PREFACE

Sixteen years ago I edited a call to church planting entitled *Multiplying Churches*.[1]

Things were very different back then. There were just over 361 million internet users. Today there are nearly ten times as many. Internet usage in Africa has increased by a staggering 7,146 per cent and globally the number of emails has increased from 12 billion to over 205 billion a day. In 2000 the latest iMac computer had a processing speed of 500 MHz and weighed 17.2kg. In 2015 the iPhone 6s had a processing speed of 1.84 GHz and weighs just 143g. In 1999

---

1. Steve Timmis (ed.), *Multiplying Churches: Reaching Today's Communities through Church Planting* (Christian Focus, 2000).

there were twenty-three blogs on the internet. Wordpress and Tumblr didn't even exist. Now they host 76 million and 261 million blogs respectively. Today there are 178 million more mobile phones in the United States than there were in 2000 and the number of mobile phones now exceeds the number of people. In 2000 Facebook, iPhone, YouTube, and Wikipedia weren't even words. And Pluto was still a planet.

What has also changed dramatically in these intervening years is the attitude to church planting. When we first wrote *Multiplying Churches* the case for church planting still had to be made. Not everyone was convinced of its merit, never mind necessity. But now? Church planting is almost as common as birds in an aviary. Which begs the question, why a new edition of the book? There are five important reasons.

First, when something is common practice – perhaps *especially* when something is common practice – it is vital that the principles that prompted it are revisited and re-evaluated. And often! Otherwise pragmatism will creep into our practice and our psyche, no matter how principled the initiative was in the beginning.

Second, something that has become established can all too easily become *passé*. Church planting is now no big deal, and so many of the radicals and activists among us have moved on, looking to ride the next emerging wave.

Third, the world has moved on and the need is now even greater than it was at the start of this millennium. A staggering 1.2 billion people have been born since the start of the new millennium. Only 15 per cent of people born between 1980 and 2000 could be classified as 'Christian'.

Four, because church planting has become 'normal', so much more experience can be drawn on to inform how we go forward. Lessons have been learned; mistakes made; victories secured. Not to disseminate such learning would be remiss – especially when all those involved in writing this book have been actively involved in the task, some for the entire period.

Five, Jesus has not yet returned. The fact that you are reading this book means that is still the case. So the command to 'Go and make disciples of all the nations' is still in force. It has not yet been rescinded. Church planting is the most effective means of obeying that command and achieving the end.

This book is not an updated version of the book we wrote in 2000. The core convictions remain the same and some material has been reused. But most of the content is new. That's because we've learnt important lessons. But it's also because we face new challenges today. Consider some sobering trends that have emerged from a range of research projects:[2]

- Notwithstanding all the additions, a net 66 million people are expected to 'leave' Christianity by 2050.

- In North America there are projected to be 27 million fewer Christians by 2050 than in 2010.

2. Pew Research Centre, 'The Future of World Religions: Population Growth Projections, 2010-2050' (April 2015), pp. 41, 43, 47, 50, 70; D. Thomson, '2067: the End of British Christianity' in The Spectator (June 2015), <http://new.spectator.co.uk/2015/06/2067-the-end-of-british-christianity>, accessed on 4 December 2015.

- An estimated 19 million people moved across international borders between 2010 and 2015, including an inflow of 1 million Muslims to Europe.

- Islam is projected to account for 11.8 per cent of the U.K. population in 2050.

- Globally the Muslim population is growing twice as fast as the overall population.

- If current trends were to continue as they are then Anglicanism in the U.K. will disappear in 2033, and 2067 would see the end of British Christianity altogether!

Of course, as Mark Twain famously said: 'There are three kinds of lies: lies, damned lies, and statistics.' So we are right to be cautious about some of these projections. Yet ignorance is more often foolishness than it is bliss. So we cannot hide our heads in the sand. We need to be aware of the situation the global church is facing.

What should our response be to these somewhat pessimistic statistics?

Despair? That would be an understandable response at one level. The picture does look bleak. Yet belief in a sovereign God makes such a reaction not only implausible, but actually sinful!

Apathy? An apathy towards the picture these numbers paint is only possible if you also have a deep apathy towards God and His glory.

Action? Surely this has to be the response of those in whom the Spirit of God dwells. He is not passive or pessimistic – and neither should we be.

It's often said that the only way to defeat the darkness is to light more candles. This is precisely what church planting is. Church planting is the act of creating communities of light across this dark world. And this is what our Lord calls us to do with the promise that He will build His church so that the gates of hell cannot prevail against it (Matt. 16:18).

This is a book created by practitioners who are involved in Acts 29, a diverse, global family of church-planting churches. It is our prayer that you will not only be encouraged but also challenged; comforted but also rebuked; informed but also equipped. But our prayer is bigger and bolder than even that. Our prayer is that out of this book, new congregations of God's people will be born and new momentum gained. David Garrison says: 'Without exaggeration we can say that church planting movements are the most effective means in the world today of drawing lost millions into saving, disciple-building relationships with Jesus Christ.'[3] May the Lord give us such movements, and may this book make a contribution to their birth and development.

STEVE TIMMIS
Executive Director
Acts 29

3. David Garrison, *Church Planting Movements* (Midlothian: Wigtake Resources, 2003), p. 28.

CONTRIBUTORS

Henri Blocher
Henri Blocher is Guenther H. Knoedler Chair of Theology at Wheaton College in Wheaton, Illinois, and Professor of Systematic Theology at the Faculté Libre de Théologie Évangélique, Vaux-sur-Seine, France. His books include *Original Sin, Evil and the Cross* and *In the Beginning*.

Matt Chandler
Matt Chandler is the founder and lead pastor of The Village Church, Texas, and President of Acts 29. His books include *The Explicit Gospel, To Live Is Christ to Die Is Gain* and *Creature of the Word*.

Tim Chester
Tim Chester is a pastor with Grace Church, Boroughbridge, U.K., and a tutor with the Acts 29 Oak Hill Academy. He is the author of over thirty books.

Reuben Hunter
Reuben Hunter is the lead planter at Trinity West, a church plant in west London. He was previously a pastoral intern with Capital Hill Baptist Church, Washington D.C. and assistant pastor at Spicer Street Church, St. Albans, U.K.

One Mokgatle
One Mokgatle is the lead planter of Rooted Fellowship, a transcultural church in Pretoria, South Africa. A graduate in corporate law, One worked with Campus Outreach before training as a church planter.

Steve Timmis
Steve Timmis is executive director of Acts 29 and the founding pastor of The Crowded House, Sheffield, U.K. His books include *Gospel-Centred Leadership, I Wish Jesus Hadn't Said That* and *Total Church*.

Ruth Woodrow
Ruth is a founding member of The Crowded House, Loughborough, U.K., and the mother of four children. She is married to Jonny, an Acts 29 church planter.

1

Let there be light: church planting and the story of the Bible

TIM CHESTER

We live in a dark world. For all our technological advances and increased prosperity, the social fabric in the West is fragmenting. More marriages than ever end in divorce and in its wake divorce brings family break-up. Mental health problems are higher than ever. Viewed from the perspective of the gospel Europe is now the dark continent. The ten mega-peoples least responsive to the gospel are all found in Europe according to the World Christian Database.[1] A report by Greater Europe Mission concludes: 'Although Europe has a high percentage of people who consider themselves Christians, the data shows that Europe has the least population percentage of Christians who consider themselves committed and evangelical.'[2] Europe is the world's most secular continent.

What is the solution to darkness? The answer, of course, is light. So it is striking that God's first words in the Bible story are, 'Let there be light' (Gen. 1:3). The context is the darkness of the primordial chaos. God had created the heavens and earth, but 'the earth was without form and void, and darkness was over the face of the deep' (Gen. 1:2). Into the darkness, God speaks and the result is light.

In the ancient world the great lights of the sky – the stars and planets – were often deified. But in the Bible's account of creation they are created. It is God who is the ultimate source of light (Pss. 18:28; 118:27; Acts 22:6-11; 1 Tim. 6:16; 1 John 1:5). God Himself is clothed in light: 'covering yourself with light as with a garment' (Ps. 104:2; Matt. 17:2). Psalm 139:12 says: 'even the darkness is not dark to you; the night is bright as the day, for darkness is as light with you.' Where God is, there is light so that even night shines like day. God is sometimes said to be clothed in darkness, but in context this

---

1. Cited in Greater Europe mission, 'European Christian Demographics', <www.joshuaproject.net/assets/unreachedeurope.pdf>. The least responsive mega-peoples are Swedish, Russian, Lithuanian, Polish, Georgian, Serb, French, Irish, Czech and Italian.

2. Greater Europe mission, 'European Christian Demographics', <www.joshuaproject.net/assets/unreachedeurope.pdf>.

simply means He is hidden from the view of human beings (Exod. 20:21; 2 Sam. 22:10, 12; 1 Kings 8:12; Ps. 97:2). So, instead of the sun, moon and stars being worshipped by human beings, the Bible calls on the sun, moon and stars to praise God: 'Praise him, sun and moon, praise him, all you shining stars ... Let them praise the name of the LORD, for he commanded and they were created.' (Ps. 148:3, 5)

'And God said, "Let there be light," and there was light.' (Gen. 1:3) God's creative and missional purpose is to overcome darkness and chaos. Light is a solution to both. How light solves the problem of darkness is clear. When you wake in the middle of night and want to navigate your way to the bathroom, you turn on the light. Light dispels darkness.

But light is also connected with overcoming chaos. The account of the fourth day of creation reads:

> And God said, 'Let there be lights in the expanse of the heavens to separate the day from the night. And let them be for signs and for seasons, and for days and years, and let them be lights in the expanse of the heavens to give light upon the earth.' And it was so. And God made the two great lights – the greater light to rule the day and the lesser light to rule the night – and the stars. (Gen. 1:14-16)

Notice the word 'rule'. The sun is made to 'rule' the day and the moon is made to the 'rule' the night.

The problem with the earth, according to verse 2, is twofold: it is without form and it is void. The creative activity of God overcomes these two problems. In days one to three God forms what is without form. The word 'separate' is used repeatedly to describe this activity. God separates what was previously chaotically mixed. Also on the first three days God names – an activity He will hand to human beings as part of their mandate to rule the earth. God rules the chaos. On days four to six God fills what was a void. He fills the sky with stars on day four. He fills the waters and skies with sea creatures and birds on day five. He fills the land with animals on day six.

Then, when God makes human beings, He hands on this creative activity. We are given this same twofold task. 'And God blessed them. And God said to them, "Be fruitful and multiply and fill the earth and subdue it, and have dominion over the fish of the sea and over the birds of the heavens and over every living thing that moves on the earth."' (Gen. 1:28) We are to fill and we are to subdue. We are to be fruitful and we are to rule. In the image of God, we are to fill what is empty and rule what is chaotic.

So the use of the term 'rule' in verse 16 to describe the role of the sun and moon is not incidental. It reflects a major theme of Genesis 1. The spread of light is the spread of order.

We know this from our own experience. The night is a time of fear and frights. Without light we cannot locate our way or perform basic tasks. Darkness is also a cover for crime so that the night is associated with evil and threat. The night is 'unruly' and therefore dangerous. Jesus says: 'For everyone who does wicked things hates the light and does not come to the light lest his works should be exposed.' (John 3:20) To belong to the night is to be *un*ruly or to belong to *mis*rule. In contrast, to live under God's rule is to live in the light (Prov. 4:18; Rom. 13:12).

Darkness is also a symbol of judgment (Isa. 13:10; 59:9; Jer. 13:16; 25:10; Lam. 3:2; Ezek. 32:7-8; Amos 5:18-20; Matt. 24:29; Rev. 18:23). One of the plagues on Egypt was the plague of darkness: 'So Moses stretched out his hand towards heaven, and there was pitch darkness in all the land of Egypt for three days. They did not see one another, nor did anyone rise from his place for three days.' (Exod. 10:22-23) This is the penultimate plague: the extinction of light is second only to the extinction of life. Indeed light and life are often connected. Psalm 13:3, for example, says: 'Light up my eyes, lest I sleep the sleep of death.' (See also Pss. 36:9; 38:10; 49:19; 56:13; Isa. 53:11.) Jeremiah 4 describes God's coming judgment as an act of de-creation that will undo what was done at creation. The birds will fly away. The land will become a desert. Jeremiah says: 'I looked on the earth, and behold, it was without form and void; and to the heavens, and they had no light.' (Jer. 4:23) We are back in Genesis 1:2. He goes on: '[For] this earth shall mourn, and the heavens above be dark; for I have spoken; I have purposed; I have not relented, nor will I turn back.' (Jer. 4:28) At creation God spoke and there was light. Now in judgment God speaks and there is darkness: 'the heavens above be dark, *for I have spoken*.' Hell is repeatedly described as a place of darkness (Matt. 8:12; 22:13; 25:30; 2 Pet. 2:4, 17; Jude 1:6, 13).

Light through the word of God

So God's creative and missional purpose is to overcome chaos and dispel darkness by bringing light. But how does He do this? Through His word. This is what brings light in the story of creation. 'And God *said*, "Let there be light," and there was light.' (Gen. 1:3) God's word is a light-bringing word.

Light and dark are not locked in a dualistic battle. Again ancient cultures often viewed the universe in these terms. Chaos and order, darkness and light, were held to be in a perpetual and precarious balance. But this is not the picture presented in the Bible story. Darkness is a genuine threat. But God dispels the darkness simply by His word. And God is sovereign even over darkness and disorder. In Isaiah 45:7 God says: 'I form light and create darkness, I make well-being and create calamity; I am the LORD, who does all these things.'

We know from our own experience that light and darkness are asymmetrical. Light dispels darkness simply by its presence whereas darkness does not naturally extinguish light. You cannot have a 'torch-dark' that casts a beam of darkness into the light. But a 'torch-light' casts a beam of light into the darkness.

So the first divine words of the Bible are programmatic for the whole story. 'And God said, "Let there be light," and there was light.' (Gen. 1:3) Wherever and whenever God speaks, the result is light:

- 'Your word is a lamp to my feet and a light to my path.' (Ps. 119:105)

- 'The unfolding of your words gives light.' (Ps. 119:130)

- 'For the commandment is a lamp and the teaching a light, and the reproofs of discipline are the way of life.' (Prov. 6:23)

- 'And we have something more sure, the prophetic word, to which you will do well to pay attention as to a lamp shining in a dark place, until the day dawns and the morning star rises in your hearts.' (2 Pet. 1:19)

The opposite is also true. 'If they will not speak according to this word, it is because they have no dawn.' (Isa. 8:20) Where God's word is absent, darkness closes back in (Ps. 82:5; Eccles. 2:13-14). And those who 'walk in darkness' are those who 'do not practise the truth' (1 John 1:6).

In Exodus 34 we read: 'When Moses came down from Mount Sinai, with the two tablets of the testimony in his hand as he came down from the mountain, Moses did not know that the skin of his face shone because he had been talking with God. Aaron and all the people of Israel saw Moses, and behold, the skin of his face shone, and they were afraid to come near him.' (Exod. 34:29-30) God is often described as radiant. Psalm 76:4 (NIV) says: 'You are radiant with light.' Now Moses is described as radiant. Moses encounters God and it seems that as a result some of God's radiance has rubbed off on him. He is glowing with the light of God. It is easy for us to think of this in visual terms. If you heat something up then it glows and emits light.

But the text does not say Moses was radiant because he had seen God. Indeed in the previous chapter Moses asks to see God and is told 'you cannot see my face, for man shall not see me and live' (Exod. 33:20). Instead, in chapter 33, God proclaims His Name to Moses. And here in chapter 34 the face of Moses is radiant, we are told, 'because he had *been talking* with God' (34:29). It is the word of the LORD that brings light. 'The commandment of the LORD is pure,' says David in Psalm 19:8, 'enlightening the eyes.'

Light through the people of God

So God brings light through His word. But He also brings light through His people.

The story of redemption really gets going with God's promise to Abraham. God promises Abraham a people who will enjoy God's blessing and a place of blessing. But God also gives this people a missional mandate right from the beginning. He promises that through Abraham's family 'all the families of the earth shall be blessed' (Gen. 12:3). This is the point in the story where God focuses down on one person, one family and one nation. But right from the beginning God says that His purposes for Abraham and Israel are for the sake of the nations. So much so that when Paul wants to defend his mission to the 'Gentiles' or 'nations' (it is the same word in Greek) he does not turn to the Great Commission – though he might have done. He turns instead to the Old Testament and to the promise of God to Abraham: 'And the Scripture, foreseeing that God would justify the Gentiles [= the nations] by faith, preached the gospel beforehand to Abraham, saying, "In you shall all the nations be blessed." ... if you are Christ's, then you are Abraham's offspring, heirs according to promise.' (Gal. 3:8, 29) The promise to Abraham of blessing to the nations is Paul's mandate for mission (see also Rom. 1:1-6; 9:24-29; 16:25-27; Eph. 3:1-6).

And how will God bless the nations through Abraham? A central element of the answer is that the Saviour will come from the offspring of Abraham. But there is more to it than this. In Genesis 18:18 God says: 'all the nations of the earth shall be blessed in [Abraham].' Then he says: 'For I have chosen him, that he may command his children and his household after him to keep the way of the LORD by doing righteousness and justice, so that the LORD may bring to Abraham what he has promised him.' (Gen. 18:19) Notice the word 'for'. God will bring about what He has promised and what He has promised is blessing for all nations. And how will He bring about this promise? 'I have chosen him, that he may command his children and his household after him to keep the way of the LORD by doing righteousness and justice.' It is as Abraham's family lives the way of the LORD that God will bless all nations. God's people are to be passionate about justice. We are to 'do' justice, says God. And as God's people live under God's rule and walk in God's way, by doing justice so we commend God to the nations.

People think God's rule is bad news. They think God is a tyrant. They think they are better off governing their own lives without God. So our job as God's people is to live in such a way that we show that it is good to know God and good to live under His rule. This theme keeps coming back again and again in the Bible story. It is central to what it means to be God's people and what it means to do His mission.

Numbers 6:22-27 records the words of blessing Aaron and his sons are to use. Through these words God says He will 'put my name on the people of Israel' (6:27). These are the words that mark out God's people as God's people. At the heart of that blessing are the words, 'the LORD make his face to shine upon you and be gracious to you.' God Himself is light and He brings us light when He turns His face towards us. In Psalm 4:6 David prays: 'Lift up the light of your face upon us, O LORD!' His face lights up, we might say, when He looks on His people. And He lights up His people with His smile. We meet the blessing of Aaron again in Psalm 67:

> May God be gracious to us and bless us
> > and make his face to shine upon us,
> that your way may be known on earth,
> > your saving power among all nations.
> Let the peoples praise you, O God;
> > let all the peoples praise you!
> Let the nations be glad and sing for joy,
> > for you judge the peoples with equity
> > and guide the nations upon earth.
> Let the peoples praise you, O God;
> > let all the peoples praise you!
> The earth has yielded its increase;
> > God, our God, shall bless us.
> God shall bless us;
> > let all the ends of the earth fear him!

This is the language of the Aaronic blessing. But notice what happens when God blesses His people: His ways are made known to the nations and the nations are glad. The light of God shines upon His people and that light radiates throughout the earth bringing light to the darkness and order to the chaos.

During the reign of Solomon we see Israel being a light to the nations. The Queen of Sheba travels from the ends of the world to hear God's wisdom from Solomon (1 Kings 10:1-13). The nations bring their wealth to enrich God's people and God's temple (1 Kings 10:14-29). 'People of all nations came to hear the wisdom of Solomon, and from all the kings of the earth, who had heard of his wisdom.' (1 Kings 4:34)

But Solomon also marries foreign wives who bring their foreign gods (1 Kings 11:1-3). Solomon himself joins in their worship (11:4-8). Mingled in with the theme of Israel as a light to the nations is another theme: Israel threatened by the nations. Israel's calling is to draw the nations to the way of the Lord. Israel's danger is that she will be drawn to the ways of the nations.

And this is what happens. Instead of being a light to the nations, Israel followed the ways of the nations (1 Kings 14:24; 2 Kings 16:3; 17:8, 11, 15, 33; 21:2). The nation reaches the point of no return under the reign of King Manasseh. The people do not listen to the word of God (2 Kings 21:7-9a). Instead, 'Manasseh led them astray, to do more evil than the nations had done whom the Lord destroyed before the people of Israel.' (2 Kings 21:9b) They are no longer a light to the nations. They do not even follow the ways of the nations. They are actually more evil than the nations.

So the prophets look beyond judgment to a time when God's people will again be a light to the nations. And no prophet expounds the theme of coming light more than Isaiah (Isa. 50:10; 51:4; 58:8-10).

The word that Isaiah son of Amoz saw concerning Judah
and Jerusalem:
It shall come to pass in the latter days
that the mountain of the house of the LORD
shall be established as the highest of the mountains,
and shall be lifted up above the hills;
and all the nations shall flow to it,
and many peoples shall come and say:
'Come, let us go up to the mountain of the LORD,
to the house of the God of Jacob,
that he may teach us his ways
and that we may walk in his paths.'
For out of Zion shall go the law,
and the word of the LORD from Jerusalem.
He shall judge between the nations
and shall decide disputes for many peoples;
and they shall beat their swords into ploughshares,
and their spears into pruning-hooks;
nation shall not lift up sword against nation,
neither shall they learn war any more. (Isa. 2:1-4)

Jerusalem was built on a hill. Isaiah says one day it will become the highest mountain. In other words, everyone will be able to see God's people and as a result the nations will stream into Jerusalem. The nations will want to be taught the law of God because they recognise that God is good and His rule is good, just as Moses promised in Deuteronomy 4:5-8. They will come to live under God's reign. In response to this wonderful vision, Isaiah's exhortation is this: 'O house of Jacob, come, let us walk in the light of the LORD.' (Isa. 2:5) Be a light to the nations. For the nations will come to God as God's people walk in His light.

Isaiah 9 describes the coming of God's Messiah to His people as the coming of light.

> But there will be no gloom for her who was in anguish. In the former time he brought into contempt the land of Zebulun and the land of Naphtali, but in the latter time he has made glorious the way of the sea, the land beyond the Jordan, Galilee of the nations.

> The people who walked in darkness
>   have seen a great light;
> those who dwelt in a land of deep darkness,
>   on them has light shone. (Isa. 9:1-2)

What is the light? 'For to us a child is born, to us a son is given; and the government shall be upon his shoulder, and his name shall be called Wonderful Counsellor, Mighty God, Everlasting Father, Prince of Peace.' (Isa. 9:6)

Isaiah 60 picks up this idea that God will come to His people bringing light.

> Arise, shine, for your light has come,
>   and the glory of the LORD has risen upon you.
> For behold, darkness shall cover the earth
>   and thick darkness the peoples;
> but the LORD will arise upon you,
>   and his glory will be seen upon you.
> And nations shall come to your light,
>   and kings to the brightness of your rising. (Isa. 60:1-3)

The LORD rises upon His people like the sun rising over the land so that the darkness of night is dispelled. The darkness that signifies judgment is replaced by the glory of the LORD. The prophet tells us to do two things. He tells us to do 'behold'. Look around you. Behold a world in darkness under judgment without the light of God's word. But he also says, 'Arise, shine'. What happens when God's light shines on God's people? God's people shine. 'Nations shall come to your light, and kings to the brightness of your rising.'

Isaiah 60 continues: 'Lift up your eyes all around, and see; they all gather together, they come to you; your sons shall come from afar, and your daughters shall be carried on the hip.' (Isa. 60:4) This is happening in the mission of the church. The nations are coming into the kingdom of God. 'Lift up your eyes.' Marvel at what God is doing around the world through His people. 'Then you shall see and be radiant; your heart shall thrill and exult.' (Isa. 60:5) Isaiah's vision of gospel advance builds until we read:

> The sun shall be no more
> your light by day,
>   nor for brightness shall the moon
> give you light;
> but the LORD will be your everlasting light,
>   and your God will be your glory.
> Your sun shall no more go down,
>   nor your moon withdraw itself;
> for the LORD will be your everlasting light,
>   and your days of mourning
>   shall be ended.   (Isa. 60:19-20)

The glory of God shines upon His people. Through His people it spreads throughout the earth. It spreads throughout the earth until the day comes when we no longer need the sun and moon because 'the LORD will be your everlasting light and your days of mourning shall be ended.' This idea is picked up in Revelation 21-22 in John's vision of the new creation: 'Night will be no more. They will need no light of lamp or sun, for the Lord God will be their light' (Rev. 22:5; 21:11, 23-24).

In the meantime, the people of God look to God and see the light of His face shine upon them. And, lit up by the light of His glory, they in turn become a light to the nations. The light of God is extended through the people of God.

The phrase 'a light to the nations' is taken from the Servant Songs of Isaiah. Isaiah speaks of a Servant. Sometimes the Servant appears to be Israel. Sometimes the Servant appears to be an individual who rescues Israel. The Servant is the One who embodies the calling of Israel – who Israel was meant to be – and so rescues Israel. This is what God says of the Servant:

> I will take you by the hand and keep you;
> I will give you as a covenant for the people,
>   a light for the nations,
> to open the eyes that are blind,
>   to bring out prisoners from the dungeon,
> from the prison those who sit in darkness.
>
> (Isa. 42:6-7)

> I will make you as a light for the nations,
>   that my salvation may reach to the
>   end of the earth.   (Isa. 49:6)

Light through Jesus the people of God

Eight hundred years later an old man held a baby in his arms and said:

> Lord, now you are letting your servant depart in peace,
> according to your word;
> for my eyes have seen your salvation,
> that you have prepared in the presence of all peoples,
> a light for revelation to the Gentiles,
> and for glory to your people Israel.
>
> (Luke 2:29-32)

The old man was Simeon and the baby was Jesus. Simeon was saying that the baby is the Servant of the LORD, promised by Isaiah. Jesus is the glory of God rising upon God's people, lighting them up so they radiate God's glory to the nations. And He is the light of the nations. Matthew says the promise of Isaiah 9:1-2, that people walking in darkness would see a great light, is fulfilled as Jesus goes into Galilee (Matt. 4:12-17).

And then Jesus Himself stands up and says: 'I am the light of the world. Whoever follows me will not walk in darkness, but will have the light of life.' (John 8:12; 9:5; 12:46; Acts 13:47) Jesus is the servant of the LORD promised by Isaiah. He is the true people of God revealing the goodness of God's reign through His goodness of life.

In Romans 1:18–2:16 Paul shows how all humanity is enslaved by sin and under judgment. But he anticipates a Jew saying something like, 'I'm OK for I'm part of God's people because I have the law' (2:17). Ultimately in 3:9-20 Paul will show that the supposed defence witness of the law is in fact a prosecution witness. The law condemns Israel so the whole world (Jews and Gentiles) is condemned. Israel were God's interim solution to the problem of humanity's sin. They were to be a light to the nations, showing the way back to God. They were entrusted with the message of God so they might make God's righteousness known to the nations (3:2). But in 2:17-24 Paul reminds his readers what actually happened. They claimed to be 'a light to those who are in darkness' (2:19), but they broke the law they were supposed to commend. Instead of being a light to the nations, the very opposite occurred: 'For as it is written: "The name of God is blasphemed among the Gentiles because of you."' (Rom. 2:24) So to keep to plan God must provide a faithful Jew who will make God's righteousness known. And that is what God has provided in Jesus Christ. 'But now the righteousness of God has been manifested apart from the law, although the Law and the Prophets bear witness to it – the righteousness of God through faith in Jesus Christ for all who believe.' (Rom. 3:21-22) Jesus is the faithful One who reveals God's righteousness. Jesus makes God known and He makes us right with God with His substitutionary death as a propitiatory sacrifice.

Light through Jesus the word of God

Not only does Jesus bring light because He is *the true people of God*. He brings light because He is *the true Word of God*. John's Gospel begins:

> In the beginning was the Word, and the Word was with God, and the Word was God. He was in the beginning with God. All things were made through him, and without him was not

anything made that was made. In him was life, and the life was the light of men. The light shines in the darkness, and the darkness has not overcome it. (John 1:1-5)

Here is the story of creation being recapitulated. John deliberately echoes the opening of Genesis. Like Genesis he starts, 'In the beginning'. And what is in the beginning is the Word of God, the Creative Word which is God. And through this Word, God brings life and light. He brings light to the darkness. But John is no longer talking about the original creation. He is talking about the coming of Jesus. 'The true light, which enlightens everyone, was coming into the world.' (John 1:9) As at creation, the Word brings light to the darkness. And the Word is Jesus. 'I have come into the world as light,' says Jesus in John 12:46, 'so that whoever believes in me may not remain in darkness.'

The light is extinguished at the cross

John says: 'And this is the judgment: the light has come into the world, and people loved the darkness rather than the light because their deeds were evil.' (John 3:19)

During the final meal of Jesus with his disciples we read a phrase full of foreboding: 'So, after receiving the morsel of bread, [Judas] immediately went out. And it was night.' (John 13:30) John has already told us it is evening so we hardly need to know what time it is (John 13:2). So the night that Judas enters is more than merely a time of day. Earlier in John's Gospel Jesus has said: 'If anyone walks in the day, he does not stumble, because he sees the light of this world. But if anyone walks in the night, he stumbles, because the light is not in him.' (John 11:9-10) Judas is going out to walk by night. The darkness is about to fall.

As Jesus dies on the cross we read: 'Now from the sixth hour there was darkness all over the land until the ninth hour.' (Matt. 27:45) The light is extinguished. The darkness falls for judgment falls. The judgment of God falls on the people of God in the person of Jesus. And the light of God's people is extinguished.

But three days later Jesus walks out of the tomb and we walk out with Him. The night is over. The new day is dawning. We now are the people of the light. 'For you are all children of light, children of the day. We are not of the night or of the darkness.' (1 Thess. 5:5; Rom. 13:12; Col. 1:12)

Light through the word of Jesus

When he appeared before King Agrippa, Paul said the Risen Christ had commissioned him with these words: '[I am] delivering you from your people and from the Gentiles – to whom I am sending you: to open their eyes, so that they may turn from darkness to light and from the power of Satan to God, that they may receive forgiveness of sins and a place among those who are sanctified by faith in me.' (Acts 26:17-18)

The *purpose* of God's mission has not changed. God's purpose at creation was to dispel darkness by bringing light. And today the purpose of His mission is to dispel darkness by bringing light. And the *means* of God's mission has not changed. At creation God brought light by speaking His word. And today we bring light by speaking God's word.

In 2 Corinthians Paul reminds his readers of the story of Moses having to cover his face with a veil because it shone with the radiance of God. Now we are, like Moses, 'with unveiled face beholding the glory of the Lord'. And as a result we, like Moses, 'are being transformed into the same image from one degree of glory to another. For this comes from the Lord who is the Spirit' (2 Cor. 3:18). We, too, shine with the reflected radiance of God.

But how do we contemplate God's glory? Paul goes on: 'The god of this world has blinded the minds of the unbelievers, to keep them from seeing the light of the gospel of the glory of Christ, who is the image of God.' (2 Cor. 4:4) We see the glory of God in the gospel of Christ. Christ is the word of God which is spoken to us. And that word is light. That word radiates with God's glory. So Paul says we do not preach ourselves. We preach Jesus Christ as Lord (2 Cor. 4:5). Because when Jesus the Word is proclaimed something extraordinary happens. 'For God, who said, "Let light shine out of darkness," has shone in our hearts to give the light of the knowledge of the glory of God in the face of Jesus Christ.' (2 Cor. 4:6) The only parallel for what happens when someone believes the word of Jesus is what happened at creation. Creation happens all over again when someone becomes a Christian. At creation God spoke and there was light. And again God speaks and there is light. There is, as Paul says in the next chapter, an act of new creation (2 Cor. 5:17).

The One who speaks and there is light, speaks to us. The One who addresses a word to the darkness and brings forth light, who addresses the chaos and brings beauty, who addresses the emptiness and brings forth this world in all its fulness, addresses a word to us. And that word is Jesus. And His word brings light. Through the preaching of Jesus God 'has shone in our hearts to give us the light of the knowledge of the glory of God in the face of Christ.'

Light through the people of Jesus

Jesus says to his disciples:

> You are the light of the world. A city set on a hill cannot be hidden. Nor do people light a lamp and put it under a basket, but on a stand, and it gives light to all in the house. In the same way, let your light shine before others, so that they may see your good works and give glory to your Father who is in heaven. (Matt. 5:14-16)

The community of Jesus is to be the light to the world that Israel failed to be. They are the city on a hill to which the nations will flow as Isaiah promised (Isa. 2:1-5). The community of Jesus embodies Isaiah's vision of peace and justice. And just as Isaiah's application was a call to walk in the light of the LORD (Isa. 2:5), so Jesus' application is to 'let your light shine before others'. And He promises that as we do, people 'see your good works and give glory to your Father who is in heaven' (Matt. 5:16).

In a similar vein Paul says:

> For at one time you were darkness, but now you are light in the Lord. Walk as children of light (for the fruit of the light is found in all that is good and right and true), and try to discern

what is pleasing to the Lord. Take no part in the unfruitful works of darkness, but instead expose them. For it is shameful even to speak of the things that they do in secret. But when anything is exposed by the light, it becomes visible, for anything that becomes visible is light. Therefore it says:

> 'Awake, O sleeper,
>   and arise from the dead,
>   and Christ will shine on you.' (Eph. 5:8-14)

We are the community of light in contrast to the community of darkness in Ephesians 6:12. What does this mean for us today? What does this have to do with church planting?

We are communities of light

First, we are communities of light. Mission is not something we achieve. It is part of our identity. Mission is central to what it means to be God's people. For many people mission has become an event. There is nothing wrong with missional events. They are an important part of the life of any church. But we cannot reduce mission to events or activities we put into our schedules. Mission is more than this. It is an identity and a lifestyle. It is about living all of life, ordinary life, with gospel intentionality.

The challenge to us is that of Matthew 5:15: 'Nor do people light a lamp and put it under a basket, but on a stand, and it gives light to all in the house.' Our light must be seen. Our lives must be transparent. We need to be out there in the world. We need to be introducing our unbelieving friends to our Christian friends. We must be reaching out beyond the community, welcoming others and pointing them to the Father.

But we are not simply called to be individual lights for Jesus. This is not a matter of lone Christians living godly lives and doing good works. We are *communities* of light. We are called to missional *community*. In the Old Testament it was the life of the covenant community which was to function as a light to the nations. And in the New Testament, too, it is the life of the community that commends the gospel. After Jesus has given the new commandment to His disciples to love one another as He has loved them, He says: 'By this all people will know that you are my disciples, if you have love for one another.' (John 13:35) Our love for one another reveals our identity and the gospel that gives us our identity. Jesus prays that those who believe in the gospel might 'all be one, so that the world may believe that you have sent me and loved them even as you loved me.' (John 17:20-23) The world will know that Jesus is the Son of God sent by God to be Saviour of the world through the community of believers. The invisible God is made visible through the love of the Christian community (1 John 4:12).

The world lives according to the lie of Satan, believing that God's reign is tyrannical. Jesus began His ministry proclaiming the good news of the kingdom of God. But most people do not hear this as good news. That is because from Eden onwards we have believed the lie of Satan. The Serpent's lie in the Garden was that God's rule was harsh and tyrannical. Believing the lie, humanity rejects God's rule.

But God's people are called to so live in obedience to God's word that they demonstrate the reign of God to be the liberating, loving and life-giving reign that it is. The nations will see that it is good to have God 'near' you (Deut. 4:5-8). This is an apologetic that goes to the heart of the matter – literally. It addresses the rebellion of the human heart. The lie that rules our hearts is that God's reign is tyrannical. So God's people are called to be a light to the nations, demonstrating that the lie is a lie and that the truth is that God is good and His rule brings freedom.

This does not simply mean inviting people to meetings. If we think of church simply as an event, then being a community of light will simply become inviting people to events. But we are not called to create 'meetings of light' or 'events of light'. We ourselves are the light. We are called to be *communities of light*. It is about a shared life that reflects the gospel into which other people are welcomed.

One of the key rationales for church planting is this: *church planting puts the Christian community at the heart of mission.* If individuals were at the heart of God's purposes then it would be quite natural to put the individual at the heart of mission. But at the heart of God's plan of salvation are a family and a nation. And so the church should be at the heart of mission. Together we demonstrate the reconciling power of the gospel. Our different life experiences give texture and colour to our message. Our diverse gifts complement one another. We show that life together under the reign of God is the good life. The church should be at the heart of mission, and that happens naturally and inevitably when you are church planting.

We are scattered communities of light

It is often said that mission in the Old Testament was centripetal (inwards, towards the centre), but that mission in the New Testament is now centrifugal (outwards, from the centre).

Clearly mission in the New Testament is centrifugal and in a way that was not the case so much in the Old Testament. We are to 'go and make disciples of all nations' (Matt. 28:19). And yet at the same time mission in the New Testament has not ceased to be centripetal. As we have seen, we are called to be communities of light that draw people to the reign of God. What has changed is the centre. The nations no longer stream into a literal city of Jerusalem. They are drawn to the new Jerusalem – to the church. We are the new Jerusalem, the city on the hill. So now mission involves a double movement. Jesus sends us out to the ends of the earth and everywhere we go we create communities of light that draw people in.

I once saw a video which depicted the explosive growth of the world's population. The video showed a spinning globe in which cities of one million people were represented by a dot of light. The globe spun and a clock in the corner marked the passage of time. For centuries there were just one or two dots of light. Then in the twentieth century the globe burst into light. Light filled whole continents.

Think of churches as dots of light. Our job is to go out into the world and establish communities that enable people to see and to share the life of Christ. We litter the world with little communities of light so that neighbourhoods, regions and countries burst into light.

We have seen that one of the key rationales for church planting is that church planting puts the Christian community at the heart of mission. The other key rationale is the converse of this: *church planting puts mission at the heart of the Christian community.*

A friend of mine became a Christian in his twenties. He was a merchant seaman and had never been to church until he was converted. He tells how he was so excited about his first church business meeting. He had been to a few Sunday meetings and been baptized. Now his first quarterly church meeting was coming up. And he was really looking forward to it. This, as he puts it, was where they were going to plot the downfall of Satan. He was in for a big shock. He discovered the main issue for discussion was the type of toilet paper they should have in the toilets. It was a big disappointment!

Mission very easily becomes one activity in church life among others. It sits on the agenda alongside a list of other items, vying with them for attention. Or it is left to the enthusiasts to get on with at the edge of church life. For other churches mission seems a distant dream as they struggle to keep the institution of church afloat.

But church planting inevitably and naturally shifts the church into missionary mode. Church planting ensures that mission defines the nature, purpose and activity of the church – as it should.

So church planting is the point where mission and church intersect. Church planting is by definition a missionary activity, arguably *the* core missionary activity. It ensures mission is at the heart of church life. But church planting is by definition a church activity. It ensures that church is integral to mission. It defines mission as forming and building churches. Church planting puts mission at the heart of church and church at the heart of mission.

Christ died for His bride, the church. I am saved when by faith I become part of the people for whom Christ died. My identity as a Christian is a communal identity. We are called to community. But we are not simply called to community for our own benefit. We are communities of light, designed by God to fulfil His mission of bringing light to the darkness.

The winter evenings where I live are dark. And as you walk our cold, dark streets with houses close to the pavement you can see into people's homes. I often wonder what passers-by make of our missional communities when they look in. It creates for me a lovely image of mission. We live in a cold and dark world. But when people look in through the window they see a community of joy, love, friendship – a place of light and warmth and welcome. This is what the church must be in our dark, cold, loveless world: a community of light *at street level*. Here is the place where God's kingdom can be glimpsed. Here is where people are reconciled as they are brought together in Christ. This is the reason for church planting: to be a light to the nations at street level.

> Therefore, my beloved, as you have always obeyed, so now, not only as in my presence, but much more in my absence, work out your own salvation with fear and trembling, for it is God who works in you, both to will and to work for his good pleasure.
>
> Do all things without grumbling or questioning, that you may be blameless and innocent, children of God without blemish in the midst of a crooked and twisted generation, among whom you shine as lights in the world holding fast to the word of life. (Phil. 2:12-16)

41

2

Let us make mankind: church planting and the story of creation

HENRI BLOCHER

The Apostle Paul wrote to the church which he had planted in Corinth: 'I feel a divine jealousy for you, for I betrothed you to one husband, to present you as a pure virgin to Christ. But I am afraid that as the serpent deceived Eve by his cunning, your thoughts will be led astray from a sincere and pure devotion to Christ.' (2 Cor. 11:2-3)

What has the topic of church planting to do with the early chapters of Genesis? What has the setting up of new churches as the goal of the Christian mission in common with the revelation of cosmic origins and of the Fall, the majestic overture of the biblical symphony? At first sight, the two, in their themes and perspectives, are far removed from each other.

And yet. If the display of the Seven Days and the story of Eden are indeed, as Luther said 'the foundation of the whole Scripture,' if they build the framework in which everything else makes sense, and if church planting is no peripheral, no insignificant, part of the disciples' mandate, *there must be a link worth pondering* between the two. We even find a biblical precedent: the patron saint of church planters, the Apostle Paul, referred to Genesis 3 to admonish his Corinthian converts in 2 Corinthians 11. The challenge for us is to discern such a link, to ascertain its contours, and to suggest its import or consequences.

We are interested in the main lines, the axes of biblical truth. I will leave aside issues which may touch on the relationship between Genesis and church planting, but in a superficial, accidental, way. These might include, for instance, how should we handle a conflict of interpretation over creation and evolution in a small, initial, group, the nucleus of the church to be born? I do not intend to deal with such a problem.

1. God's intent to have a *partner* people

What is the LORD aiming at in the first place? What is the ultimate purpose on His mind when He creates a world and beings distinct from Himself? He lacks nothing at all and nothing can be added to absolute, infinite, fulness. His motive must be generosity, in the strong sense of the word. But in whose favour? The first 'tablet' of Genesis, the prologue (1:1–2:3), reveals His goal, and the second 'tablet' offers a kind of 'close-up' of the final work, followed by what happened next. (As I have shown elsewhere,[1] while both refer to real space-time beginnings, they have been composed under divine inspiration with the subtlety of the wise. They aptly charm popular imagination through semi-poetic devices, images, allusions, plays on words, and at the same time they communicate profound theological lessons.)

The construction of the first tablet leads up to the crowning work: God sets humankind in front of Him. The second tablet shows the LORD tenderly shaping them and providing for their well-being. The very distance between heaven and earth is part of a 'vis-à-vis' structure: humankind's earthliness (and this is a connotation of the name 'Adam' drawn from the *'ᵃdàmâ*, the red earth or ground) enables them to stand as 'partners' with and before God, while angels are 'too near' for such a status. They can only be flames in the eternal fire of His holiness. Being partners for God means being the objects of His care and of His command, the addressees of His precepts and promises, able and called to respond in trusting obedience. One cannot miss indications that such is God's purpose in creation.

The human privilege is defined in terms of *imaging God*. I take the Hebrew prepositions in Genesis 1:26 to mean that humans *are* God's image, His living likeness among earthly

---

1. Henri Blocher, *In the Beginning: The Opening Chapters of Genesis* (IVP, 1984).

creatures, with a polemical reference to the false *idol*-images. Just as one faces one's image in the mirror of clear waters, God is pleased to behold His own image in the mirror of His creation here below. Vice-regent's dominion granted to the human creature reflects the LORD's sovereign rule, and the structure of the man-woman relationship reflects the LORD's partnership with humankind, 'vis-à-vis' being an exact translation of the term used in Genesis 2:18.

One may also call the 'vis-à-vis' structure by the key biblical word *covenant*. Theological tradition spoke of an Edenic 'covenant of works'. To avoid misunderstandings, I prefer to say 'creational covenant', but I am happy to find the essential ingredients of covenant in the LORD's dispositions in Genesis 2:15-17. Hosea 6:7 recalls that covenant, according to the old interpretation – still the best – of this verse.

A further illustration of human partnership in God's original covenant is found in the Seventh Day. The culmination of the creative process itself is a work of the Sixth Day. Yet *it is not the end of the matter*. The Seventh Day follows, a day which does not end in Genesis (history takes place within that day according to John 5:17). This is the Day which God blesses and sanctifies for humankind – for whom else? – so that His living images will take time to respond and to enjoy their correspondence – we may say 'fellowship' – with Him. God achieves His purposes when there is a partner people who stands in front of Him to listen to His word and to answer in joyful confession and praise.

This partner *people* can be called a 'nation' for we may emphasise the organic, collective, corporate, dimension of humankind as willed by God. As is well known, the term 'Adam', before being used for the first individual, the Patriarch, is a collective noun for the whole *genus* of human beings. In Genesis 1 the blessing of multiplication immediately highlights that God has in view a family of humankind. The submission of the earth, the so-called 'cultural mandate', is not to be completed through in any other way. In Genesis 3 the consequences of the fateful perfidy of man and woman affect their descendants. It confirms that the LORD sees His partner-images as bound to one another in a partner *community*.

All this is deeply relevant to church planting. This is because the church embodies nothing less than the *restoration* of God's original purpose. The Enemy's cunning was enough to induce the treason of the first human Head, Adam. But the Son of God came to undo what the Devil had done (1 John 3:8). He is the New Adam in whom and through whom God's intention will be finally satisfied. His community is the new-creation humankind. And if He is the New Adam, the church may be considered the New Eve. Hence Paul's reference in 2 Corinthians 11:3 (cited above). A parallel may be drawn between the blessing of reproduction in Genesis 1:28 and the 'Great Commission' in Matthew 28, of which church planting is indeed an aspect.[2]

This beautifully accords with biblical typology. The eight persons in Noah's ark were a type of the church according to 1 Peter 3:20-22. The Flood itself typified the judgment and end

---

2. I thank Pastor Etienne Koning for this insight.

of the old world of corruption while the new beginning with Noah both paralleled the original creation and foreshadowed the new creation in Christ. The Eight, Noah's community, prefigured the church as the first-fruits of the new creation, also with the multiplication mandate (Gen. 9:1).

2. God's intent to give this people *victory over the Serpent*

The phrase 'new creation' may mislead some readers, for the relationship with the old one is a complex matter. It is not just another creation, *ex nihilo*, as if God was to tear to pieces the page that was soiled and started writing on another page. The new creation affects the old world. It is a work of radical purgation and renewal (as the Flood was as a type according to 2 Peter 3). What was created originally is being repaired and restored, not simply annihilated. That God saw fit to maintain His creation, despite sin and death that have disfigured its original beauty, is expounded in the doctrine of 'common grace' (see, for example, Acts 14:16-17). We find it a major teaching of Genesis 3: God maintains the human mandate and God maintains the blessing of reproduction, however painful and frustrating human efforts have become. It is in this *fallen* world that the LORD will unfold the mysteries of His Plan and reach the ends He has chosen.

The difference, the fact that the new creation is not *ex nihilo*, but rather *ex nihilismo* (from the preference for nothingness which is another name for sin, see 1 Samuel 12:21, where the Hebrew uses *tôhû*, 'nothingness'), entails new characteristics. As Genesis 3:15 makes clear, the new creation is part of a long war between God and the Serpent, between humankind and the ancient Serpent, that is the Devil. Had God simply wiped out His first creation to start all over again another one, 'somewhere else' (if this has any meaning!), then the Devil would have succeeded in his wicked enterprise. He would have thwarted God's original purpose. God forbid! So the LORD's counter-move does not annihilate the wicked world and refrains from a simple display of power. It proceeds from a transcendent wisdom, a wisdom which no human heart could devise (1 Cor. 2:8-10). So strange! God's champion, the Son of the Woman, will crush the Serpent's head. But how? At the cost of undergoing the Serpent's deadly bite. This strange way of the new creation is also why the Son's disciples are not to be taken out of this world of corruption, but, while still temporary residents in that world, are kept from evil and from the Evil One (John 17:15).

The war, in other words, is a spiritual war. Its weapons do not belong to the 'fleshly' plane (2 Cor. 10:4). The new creation is a 'supra-natural' work. For, indeed, the New Adam is no mere 'living being' as the first Adam was, but the Life-Giving Spirit (1 Cor. 15:45). Restoration goes far beyond mere restoration! And, since 'natural' reproduction or multiplication is being maintained through common grace, *another* begetting makes one a member of the new-creation humanity. It is begetting from above, from the Spirit, issuing in a supra-natural 'new birth'. Such is the import of the specific character of the *new* creation (of the old).

The connection with the Christian mission and church planting cannot escape the reader's eye. The spiritual operation through which one is born into the new-creation humankind

– which is called regeneration on God's side and conversion, repentance, coming to faith, in the individual's conscious experience – is the sought for fruit of evangelisation. Radically renewed 'living stones' thus assemble to build the church, to form the partner people of God. And this implies sharing in the Genesis 3:15 victory over the Serpent. The rest of the Woman's offspring (Rev. 12:17), who are still waging war though D-Day has already decided the outcome, *triumph* over the Serpent, the Accuser, *by the blood of the Lamb* (Rev. 12:11). At the cost of His own death, the New Adam crushed the head of him who held the power of death, the Devil. As a result: 'the children God has given' him might *go free* (Heb. 2:13-15). They can now trample on serpents and scorpions, all the Enemy's power (Luke 10:19) and they will 'soon crush Satan under [their] feet' (Rom. 16:20). Such New Testament echoes of the Genesis 3 *Protoevangelium* confirm that heralding the Gospel, testifying of Christ, persuading of biblical truth and planting churches means taking part in the long battle with the Serpent, of which the issue is certain: the victory of faith over that world which lies under the control of the Evil One (1 John 5:4, 19).

The decisive encounter took place on Calvary. Subsidiary fighting has been victoriously sustained through centuries by the rest of the Woman's seed (Rev. 12:17). But the sobering fact remains: the war is not over yet. Accordingly, the victory of faith does not consist only in coming to faith, but also in staying in the faith, persevering and growing in the faith. Accordingly also, a church planter may not neglect what happens *next*. The Apostle Paul was at pains to assist the growth of the communities he had founded and to ward off the dangers he perceived. His reference to Genesis 3 in 2 Corinthians 11 voices his concern for the church, the New Eve, in the following stages of her life. In this he surely sets an example church planters should emulate.

The danger which is in the forefront of Paul's preoccupations is that of an *adulteration* of the true Christian message. People still preach a Jesus, but not the true Jesus. They communicate a spirit, but not the Holy Spirit. They offer good news shaped to suit common tastes, but not the saving Gospel of the Cross (2 Cor. 11:4). After Christ, the Enemy raises antichrists, substitute Christs ('anti' means substitution as well as opposition).

The threat was already visible in apostolic times. How much more in our days! 'Interpretations' of Christian doctrine that borrow the form of the godly message but deny its power (2 Tim. 3:5) have grown subtler and subtler. They often sway public opinion through media glamour and academic prestige. In Genesis 3 already, the Serpent offers a counterfeit version of God's gift. He adulterates the privilege of being the image of God and makes it into 'being like God' (one may translate this as 'like gods' or 'like God'). The 'knowledge of good and evil' is best interpreted as *autonomy*, as the ability to determine what is good or right and what is evil or wrong. It can be seen as a seductive distortion of the human privilege of responsibility, the ability to appropriate the difference, as determined by God.

There has probably been no previous epoch in history when the claim to autonomy, the *self* being the ultimate arbiter of good and evil, was so widely spread as in ours. Theologies are not lacking that cultivate this false gospel. One could add to those observations drawn from Genesis, which apply to our mission today, that the Serpent figure had strong connotations in the ancient Middle-East: the emblem of occult science, of the mastery of forbidden secrets, and also, with phallic symbolism, of sexual power. Who can deny the fascination for the same around us today?

Church planting remains in line with Genesis 3 when it arms God's partner people that they may fight the good fight of faith in anti-Christian days.

3. God's intent to give this people *a place on earth*

The second tablet of biblical revelation, the Eden chapters, brings out in bold relief how the LORD first prepares and then assigns a particular place for humankind (Gen. 2:8-15). This signifies that God takes care of His elect creature beyond creation itself. He is pleased to shower His blessings on man and woman, blessings that meet their need (good to eat) and add much more (pleasing to the eye). These blessings include a suitable environment. For this feature also ratifies that human beings, being *earthly* creatures, a dimension of their created goodness, are *locally* defined.

We see today uprooted populations by millions, countless homeless individuals. Their humanity is bleeding, whether they are aware of it or not. This remains true when afflu- ence generates the rootlessness: 'jet-set' people, who possess homes everywhere and therefore nowhere, who lead vain, de-humanised, lives.

The lesson holds whatever one's interpretation of 'Eden'. St Thomas Aquinas still believed that travelling far enough eastwards one would at last fall upon the cherubim. John Calvin no longer entertained such a naive understanding (in our eyes), and reckoned that the Flood had swept away all vestiges of the primordial paradise. But he used all the available information to try to locate Eden on the map. His *Commentary on Genesis* devotes a section to that endeavour, based on the mention of the two rivers that are well-known, the rivers Tigris and Euphrates. Since there are definite hints that the Gihon should be identified with the Nile, some simply say that the Garden covered the whole region we call the Middle-East (why not?). Others prefer a more symbolic interpretation. Whatever is the case, the LORD assigns a *place* on earth to the community He just established before Himself as His covenant partner.

This, too, applies to the church. The church is no vague concomitance of souls floating in outer space. Most occurrences of the word *ekklesia* in the New Testament refer to *local* churches. Twice only do the Gospels in Greek put that word on our Lord's very lips, and the second time the local character of the community cannot be doubted (Matt. 18:17). Planting churches, which as 'planted' are necessarily local, agrees with the LORD's intention as evidenced in Genesis 2. We could boldly draw a parallel between church *planting* and the LORD God's *planting* of a 'garden' in the beginning!

This is no cheap triumph, however. Speaking of 'local' churches involves some knotty problems, both practical and theoretical. Practically, how local is 'local'? In the apostolic period, most regular meetings of Christians would take place in the *houses* of some wealthier believers, as was already the case, we are told, in diaspora Judaism. Paul writes to 'the church (singular) of God in Corinth,' but that church would be made of several house-groups who would break the bread, hear instruction and exercise spiritual gifts in various locations. These would have included the business building and habitation of Aquila and Priscilla (1 Cor. 16:19; cf. Acts 18:24-26), the residence of that influential citizen Erastus, the city-treasurer or director of public works (Rom. 16:23), and other similar places. Experts estimate that such houses could accommodate about fifty people,[3] and up to one hundred in exceptional cases.[4] Not so far from the size of many of our own 'local churches'! Yet there is one church in Corinth in Paul's eyes – though he refrains from using the singular when he writes to the Romans. In Corinth, there are both one church and several house-churches. Is there one church or are there many in our modern megalopolises?

The difficulty of circumscribing the local church today is compounded by the changes in our way of life. *Concrete*

---

3. Derek J. Tidball, 'Social Setting of Mission Churches', in Gerald F. Hawthorne & Ralph P. Martin (eds), *Dictionary of Paul and His Letters* (Downers Grove, IL/Leicester: InterVarsity Press, 1993), p. 885.

4. Bradley B. Blue, 'Architecture, Early Church', in Ralph P. Martin & Peter H. Davids (eds), *Dictionary of the Later New Testament and Its Developments* (Downers Grove IL/Leicester: InterVarsity Press, 1997), p. 93. Blue refers to the case of the so-called Palatial Mansion with the reception hall which 'could have accommodated seventy-five people' (71.5 square metres) and taken with the adjoining rooms 'about one hundred people quite comfortably'.

experiential space, and therefore nearness and distance, is not just a matter of yards and miles, but rather of possibilities of life together, encounters, mutual help. Distance, for most of us, is measured by time of transportation. We usually spend most of our days far from home. To which place or places do we belong? Family and friendship ties should not be condemned as irrelevant when we reason in 'nearness' terms. If we set our hearts on implementing the original divine intention about locality, we must be prepared to cope with a measure of uncertainty and compromise.

'Theoretically' (keeping an eye on practical outcomes), the relationship with Jesus' first use of *ekklesia* (Matt. 16:18) is not so easy to define. Actually, it has been an apple of hot discord even among Roman Catholic theologians through the last decades. *Which* is first and fundamental, the one Church universal under the Pope or the collegial reality of the 'local' churches (they use the phrase for dioceses and episcopal wards)? Universalists, in the interest of centralised government, have inspired the wording of the Vatican's Declaration *Dominus Iesus*. Localists claim a Vatican II statement.

Among evangelical Protestants the temptation of an extreme localism has not been unknown. Many nineteenth-century Baptists in America were impressed by the promoters of *Landmarkism* who denied the present existence of the Church universal. In their view, the Church comprising all Christians was only to be gathered on the Last Day.

The localist extreme hardly squares with New Testament parlance. The Apostle speaks of Christ giving Himself for the Church and continually cleansing His Bride through the word as a preparation for the wedding-feast (Eph. 5:25-27). It ignores the massive witness to the continuity with the first Covenant people (1 Pet. 2:9-10; see also Paul's reference to the 'Israel of God' in Gal. 6:16). It misses the emphasis on the One Body, the One New Man, constituted by the threefold event of the cross, the resurrection and the outpouring of the promised Spirit.

On the other hand, we should not rate local churches simply as parts, or even cells, of the big company. The local church is *the* Church of God in that place, the distinct implementation of His purpose. Paul could not, if it were not so, use the Bride and new Eve symbolism for the *local* church in Corinth when writing in 2 Corinthians 11. The Church, as the supra-natural reality of the New Creation already effective on earth, is too radically defined by the presence of Christ through the Spirit to be divided into parts in the manner of mere human organisations. The local church *is* the Church – locally.

So we should steer clear of both dangers. We must avoid the danger of celebrating the Church universal as if it existed above and prior to local churches and believers, whether as a Platonic Idea or as an Institution. And we must avoid the danger of ignoring that the local church is the Church *in union* with all other churches as the Body of Christ. The scheme drawn by the apostle Paul may help us to strike the right balance: we are the children of the heavenly Jerusalem, 'our mother' (Gal. 4:26; Rev. 12:17). 'Our citizenship is in heaven' (Phil. 3:20) and our local churches are *colonies* of that City, the Church universal (already existing), just as the city of Philippi was a colony of Rome.

The recognition of the truth of the church universal and the local churches is expressed in many ways. While the apostles were still alive, their global supervision, Paul's 'anxiety for all the churches' (2 Cor. 11:28), established a basic framework. And their legacy, the apostolic tradition or deposit (the canon of our faith), still fulfils part of this role. It was supplemented by exchanges, letters of recommendation, conferences, gestures of solidarity and assistance. Such means are available to us, often in the form of so-called parachurch organisations and inter-church associations. Church planters will be wise if they work in close associations with existing churches and unions.

4. God's intent to see in this people both *order and life*

In the Creator's original design, as revealed in the early chapters of Genesis, two features stand out significantly: *order* and *life*. So we should expect to see the reflection of these two features in the church(es), if we have been on the right track in our preceding remarks.

The first 'tablet' shows us God creating order, out of the *tôhû-wᵃbôhû* (the primordial chaos), through *separation*. The biblical God loathes confusion. So He assigns precise limits and functions. He establishes distinct domains and structures. And then, in the second series of three creative days, He calls into being the creatures who will inhabit those domains:

- The luminaries in the space that was set up by the separation of Day 1, luminaries whose movement offers an analogy of life. (The ancients commonly thought that stars were animate beings. Scripture does not say so, but avails itself of the connotation.)

- Animals *living* in water together with birds which will swarm and populate the spaces set up on Day 2.

- Earthly animals and humankind, the superior form of *life*, who will multiply on that earth which was made ready on Day 3.

There is a refinement in this structure: a second work on Day 3 anticipates the series of the next Days, for vegetation is both part of the framework of the space to be filled *and* already a living occupant of the ground. In parallel fashion, the second work of Day 4 anticipates Day 7 for humankind, as God's living image, is to enjoy the fellowship of His rest.

The duality of the themes of order and life correspond to that of the Agents of creation as suggested by the second verse of Genesis 1: the Word and the Spirit. 'God said' – speech whose symbol is the sword (Eph. 6:17; Rev. 19:15) – delimits: disentangles the confusing mixture of sensations, fixes identities, compels choices between right and wrong. *Order* is of the *Word*. The Spirit is regularly in Scripture 'the Spirit of life'. The Spirit is the Breath without which all flesh is soon doomed to expire and the mysterious power at work in the mother's womb (Eccles. 11:5 associates the *rûah* and human generation which may well be on Jesus' mind in John 3:5-8). *Life* is of the *Spirit*.

The duality is not lost in the second 'tablet'. The LORD's arrangements look tidy indeed, with the Tree of life in the centre of the garden which man is to till and guard. This sounds like preserving *order*. Through speech (he images God), man is to identify and separate the various kinds of animals, and bring out the essential difference between human beings and beasts or birds. The words of the Edenic covenant sharply separate between right and wrong. The breaking of its law leads to a well-ordered judicial procedure, with investigation first and then a verdict pronounced on each culprit. *Order*, undoubtedly.

The emphasis on *life* is no less present. It is central with the Tree in the midst of the garden, and the free access to that tree and to the others. It is suggested by the freedom of nudity between husband and wife, transparency without shame in the relationship God Himself had instituted. It is implied by Adam's act of faith, as he understood something of the LORD's promise, when he gave his wife the name 'Eve', *hawwâ*, the doublet of *hayyâ*, 'life'.

Human thinkers have often perceived order and life as opposites. Classical preferences went to order while roman-ticism protested in the name of life. Reason has a kinship with the former and life has been valued as the mysterious X which escapes rational apprehension. Such schemes ('anti-nomies') distort the biblical perspective. Upon the divine foundation and under the divine sovereignty (which human thinkers have refused clearly to confess), order and life are found together in harmony. They even imply each other. As experience confirms, disorder causes death! No one can live in chaos. I would even refine the concept. What our apostasy has produced is not 'pure' dis-order, but a deadly caricature and perversion of order: *mis*-order. Cancer illustrates what mis-order means: a mad repetition, multiplication of cells without measure and solidarity. A remark by Konrad Lorenz, the pioneer ethnologist, is worth pondering. He says a histological section of healthy tissue resembles traditional cities; that of cancerous tissue resembles our modern agglomerations. 'There is a striking analogy between the images of our suburban areas and that of a tumour.'[5] Since it has grown fantastically in power, humankind in its modern development has been able more effectively to disregard the divine order of creation, for example in the way big cities have been planned, and the outcome has been cancerous mis-order. Conversely, death creates disorder. A corpse soon enters a 'state of decomposition'. The contrast with the biblical God is glaring for He is intent on binding order and life together!

Inasmuch as life may be defined 'biologically' as a combustion (food is fuel to produce energy), a play on words that sound almost the same may be used as a symbol: *order* and *ardour* should go together.

How relevant to church planting! Young churches, and older ones too, need both the order of the Word and the life of the Spirit. They need both as implying each other: the clear pattern of sound doctrine and efficient 'church order' on the one hand, and the warmth and elasticity of healthy tissue, all the exchanges of life, on the other hand. Preoccupation with

---

5. Konrad Lorenz, *Les Huit Péchés capitaux de notre civilisation* (trans. Elizabeth de Miribel, Paris: Flammarion, 1973), p. 41. This is the French translation of Konrad Lorenz, *Die acht Todsünden der zivilisierten Menschheit* (Munich: Piper & Co.), 1973.

order must not so dominate that it stifles the new inventions of life. That will degenerate into sclerosis and final necrosis. Neither must life and ardour be measured by excitement, or excesses of exuberance. Life in depth is no noisy phenomenon, and we must not mistake fever for fervour. A biblically harmonious balance should be sought in the apportionment of ministries and in the forms of worship, and there is room for variety and adaptation.

Conclusion

Church planting, we may not forget, while it means work, also means war. For the ancient Serpent never tires of sowing seeds of disorder and mis-order. He still attempts to deceive the New Eve through distrust of the Lord's words and goodness. But cheer up! Church planting also means sharing in the victory of the Son of the Woman, and extending its application in the sure hope of fulfilment. The Son has come, and won, to raise in the presence and fellowship of the Father the partner people He decided to create, in the harmony of order and life. God's original intention shall not be frustrated.

3

You will be my witnesses: church planting and the story of the church

STEVE TIMMIS

Any consideration of church planting has to include the book of Acts, for the book of Acts is a book about church planting. The tone is set right at the beginning when Jesus says to his disciples: 'You will receive power when the Holy Spirit has come upon you, and you will be my witnesses in Jerusalem and in all Judea and Samaria, and to the end of the earth.' (Acts 1:8)

The verb *'you will be'* is in the indicative mood. It is the mood of assertion. It portrays something as being actual. So Jesus is not suggesting this as a career option for His apostles. He was not raising the mere possibility of it happening. He was not saying that this might happen if everything worked out. It is not, 'You might be my witnesses' or 'You can be my witnesses if you so choose.' Jesus was saying that this new identity would be the direct consequence of the Holy Spirit coming upon them in power. The power of the Holy Spirit would be primarily evident in them being His witnesses to the ends of the earth.

This highlights an important truth about the Holy Spirit: the Holy Spirit creates missionaries. As soon as He calls someone into the kingdom, as soon He regenerates someone with the life of Jesus, He has created a missionary.

To be continued

In the rest of the narrative in the book of Acts, Luke sets out to demonstrate the veracity of this statement by Jesus. Jesus says the apostles will be His witnesses; Luke shows that they were His witnesses. We begin to see the gospel going to the ends of the earth. The book of Acts begins in the capital of the old world, Jerusalem, and it ends in the capital of the new world, Rome.

But the story does not end in Acts 28 with the job done. The ending of Acts is opened ended. The story continues.

Paul is proclaiming the kingdom of God in Rome as Jesus said would be the case – His people are witnesses throughout the known world. But there should not be a period or full stop at the end of Acts 28. Instead there should be an ellipsis – three dots to indicate an on-going story. Luke intends us to read Acts 28:30-31 as follows: '[Paul] lived there two whole years at his own expense, and welcomed all who came to him, proclaiming the kingdom of God and teaching about the Lord Jesus Christ with all boldness and without hindrance …' To be continued.

The insatiable ambition of the gospel

We often talk about having a gospel ambition, and that is a good thing. But Luke talks about the gospel itself having an ambition. Ambition is written into the gospel. And that is an altogether better thing. Indeed our gospel ambition is only meaningful because the gospel itself has an ambition.

And the gospel's ambition is insatiable. The gospel will not be satisfied until 'the earth will be filled with the knowledge of the glory of the LORD as the waters cover the sea' (Hab. 2:14). That is the gospel's ambition.

Filling the earth

The Bible begins in Genesis 1 with the creation of the world because God's plans have always been global. God made the world because He was intent on blessing the world. The entire world has always been the object of His affection. Jesus declares us to be His witnesses 'to the end of the earth' because that is where God's affections spread. God wants to bless the entire world.

When Jesus tells us to disciple the nations at the end of Matthew's Gospel, He is expressing the heart of God for the nations (Matt. 28:18-20). God told the first man and woman to be fruitful and multiply, to fill the earth and subdue it. Now, as we saw in chapter two, Jesus says this mandate is going to be fulfilled as His followers go to the ends of the earth and make disciples. The earth is filled and subdued as we disciple the nations.

The book of Acts is built around a series of text markers, summary statements in which Luke summarizes what has gone before. The first one is Acts 6:7 where Luke says simply 'the word of God continued to increase'. This is the story that Luke is telling – the story of the movement of the gospel. The word 'increase' is translated elsewhere as 'to make fruitful'. It has the idea of organic growth and multiplication.

This growth is illustrated in the parable of the Sower (Matt. 13:1-23). Jesus is saying that, like Adam, the sower has work to do. And what he does is go to scatter the seed which represents the word of the gospel. Some of this seed falls in unproductive places, but the majority falls on good soil. We know this because there is a record harvest. The earth responds willingly to this sower. The birds, the shallow soil, and the thorns are all ultimately ineffectual. In the end there is a great harvest. Jesus the Sower goes out to sow the seed of the gospel and He is victorious. He, as it were, bestrides the earth and the earth willingly breaks out into an exuberant harvest. Jesus is saying the message of the kingdom is going to bear an incredible harvest. The purposes of God are going to be fulfilled. God is going to disciple the nations.

The second Adam will have His harvest. This should encourage us as we go out to spread the word with Him. We are those who are in Christ. We are the redeemed Adam and the restored Israel. And so we go humbly, but with confidence.

Churches planting churches

How do we do this? Primarily by planting churches. This is what we see in the book of Acts. That is the fruit of the word. The gospel is not merely something to be declared – although it certainly is that. It is also something to be demonstrated. And that happens in churches as they are planted.

This is why 'multiplying churches' is so important. Multiplying churches is 'God's mission strategy'. Yes, evangelism is important. It is an integral part of our discipleship. Worship is important. It is a glorious expression of the gospel by which our affections are captured for Christ. They are proper activities and priorities of the local church. But at some point in some way they should result in the establishment of new churches. We should be looking to plant new churches in diverse contexts so that the gospel word might produce more gospel fruit.

It has not always been seen this way.

Back in 1991 I had the temerity to speak to a group of church and denominational leaders in an erstwhile Soviet republic which had just become a newly independent nation. I spoke passionately and persuasively, making the case for church planting. I also spoke patronisingly. I was speaking to a group of men old enough to be my father, many of whom bore the marks of their faithfulness to Jesus. The first man to stand up in a question and answer time after my talk thanked me for my talk and then told me to sit down. He said: 'Young man, we have enough problems with the churches we already have without creating more problems by starting new ones.' It was not really a question and I wondered if I should point that out to him, but wisdom prevailed and I kept quiet!

Although I sympathise with his frustration, he should not have been ruled by his cynicism. The church of Jesus Christ is the fruit of Christ's death. She is the object of His affection and the means by which, through the power of the Spirit, He will secure His kingdom. This is the glory of the church.

When Paul was writing to the church at Colossae, he wrote about the gospel bearing fruit all over the world (Col. 1:6). And what was the fruit that it was bearing? It was new churches springing up just like the church in Colossae, a church that had been started by an otherwise unknown man named Epaphras. The fruit of the gospel is communities of light invading the darkness and dispelling the oppressive gloom of chaos and disorder. This is church planting and this is how glorious it is.

Church planting is not simply starting a new congregation. Church planting is not beginning a new meeting. Church planting is not opening up a new building. Church planting is the work of filling and subduing. It is the work of pushing back the thorns and thistles of Satan's tyranny. It is a glorious task to which God has called us. God in the gospel is inviting us to participate with Him to fill the earth and subdue it. As we go out to make disciples of every nation we are extending Eden, creating Edens all over the world. We are establishing places where God rules and where God walks in mercy. It is for this that we were made. This is what the first Adam forfeited. This is what the Second Adam has gloriously secured. And this is how it has always been in the kingdom of God.

First century Antioch

I want to look at three moments in church planting – three moments of a Spirit-empowered movement. We are going, as it were, to three different locations at three different points in time – Antioch in Acts 13, Geneva at the time of Calvin, and the New Creation at the ends of the ages.

At the beginning of Acts 8 persecution breaks out against the church following the martyrdom of Stephen. As a result the followers of Jesus are dispersed. Some arrive at the city of Antioch 300 miles to the north of Jerusalem. There something extraordinary and spontaneous happens. Up until this point, Luke tells us, the church had only been speaking to Jews (Acts 11:19). Now for some reason – for some Spirit-inspired reason – they begin to speak also to Greeks or Gentiles (Acts 11:20-21). As a result of their evangelism a church is planted in Antioch.

It is important to notice that a church is planted. This is what Luke tells us in Acts 11:26 in a very matter of fact sort of manner. He describes how 'the hand of the Lord was with them, and a great number who believed turned to the Lord' (Acts 11:21). He describes how Barnabas was sent to consolidate the work and was glad when he saw the evidence of the grace of God (Acts 11:23). He describes how Barnabas brought Paul to Antioch. And then Luke describes how 'for a whole year they met with the church and taught a great many people' (Acts 11:26). There is no description of the church's formation, but clearly this is what has happened.

A church has been born out of spontaneous evangelism and that is the best form of church planting there is. There is no rigmarole or fanfare, no phases to go through, no build-up to a public launch, no fundraising programme. Instead, gloriously and spontaneously, a church is born. It is so extraordinarily ordinary. It can only be a sovereign work of the Spirit of God. And that is why it is so significant.

Why does Luke tell this story for us? Why does he include this event in his narrative? There was much that happened in the time-span covered by the book of Acts that he chose not to mention. But he includes the account of the formation of the church in Antioch because he wants to demonstrate that this is what the Holy Spirit does. He plants churches. The Trinity – Father, Son and Holy Spirit – are all church planters.

And planting churches is not simply the by-product of mission. Churches are at the heart of God's missionary method. Through the preaching of Christ, God gathers people together and forms a community – a new community of God's people. Here, as it were, God creates a new Eden in the heart of Gentile Antioch. A church is planted in Antioch without the aid of the apostles, nor any initial input from the church in Jerusalem.

But there is more. For in Acts 13 we find the first organised missionary expedition launched into Gentile territory. And it comes from this new church in Antioch.

At the end of chapter 12, Luke records the gruesome expiry of Herod. Then he includes another summary statement, a reminder in Acts 12:24 that the word of God increased and multiplied. Luke deliberately juxtaposes these two events. Herod dies because of his blasphemy and arrogance, but the word of God increases. A ruler dies, but the kingdom of God extends. The fame of Jesus keeps on getting more famous.

Then this spontaneously-planted church in Antioch becomes a church-planting church by sending out two of its best. While the leaders of the church are gathered together, the Holy Spirit says: 'Set apart for me Barnabas and Saul for the work to which I have called them' (Acts 13:2). What is that work? Church planting. Paul and Barnabas head off to plant churches in Pisidian Antioch, Iconium, Lystra and Derbe.

This church-planting expedition was launched from this spontaneously-planted church by the Holy Spirit. This is why it is so significant. A church is planted because that is what the Holy Spirit does. And then the Holy Spirit directs the church that He has planted to be the means by which He will continue the same work of planting churches.

Every church should be a church-planting church; every church without exception. Church planting is not just for those that have a special interest or capacity. Just as every believer is called to be a missionary, so every church is a church-planting church. That is because, as the Holy Spirit gathers people who are all missionaries, you have a missionary church. And a missionary church plants churches. The Spirit is a church-planting Spirit. Church planting is the preferred divine method of evangelism, of kingdom expansion, of fruit-bearing, of discipleship-making, of men and women being rescued from darkness to light.

Before his death Jesus assured His disciples of His determination to build His church. 'I will build my church,' He promised (Matt. 16:18). The story of the church is the story of the seeding, germination and growth of groups of Christians who are worshipping, learning and witnessing together. In other words, church history from Matthew 28 onwards and from Acts 28 onwards is fundamentally about church planting.

Sixteenth-century Geneva

So let us look at another moment in that story. I want to suggest that the commitment of Acts 29 to assessment, coaching, training and support is taken straight from John Calvin's Genevan church-planting manual.

There was an Englishman by the name of John Bale who found his way to Geneva as a refugee in the spiritual and political upheaval that was occurring in Europe at the time. This is what he found:

> Geneva seems to me to be the wonderful miracle of the whole world. For so many from all countries come here as it were to a sanctuary. It's wonderful that Spaniards and Italians and Scots and Englishmen and Frenchmen and Germans disagreeing in manners, speech and apparels should live so lovingly and friendly, and dwell together like a Christian congregation.[1]

Since Geneva was French-speaking, the majority of refugees in the city came from France. In Geneva they sat under the

---

1. Cited in John T. McNeill, *The History and Character of Calvinism* (OUP, 1954), pp. 178-9.

teaching of John Calvin in the Cathedral of Saint Pierre. As they listened to him opening the gospel, their hearts were stirred for their homeland. They felt compelled to return with the gospel.

But Calvin did not want to send them back as uneducated missionaries. He believed a good missionary or church planter had to be a good theologian. So Calvin tested their preaching ability. There was an assessment process in which he scrutinised their moral character. So he only sent back to France trained and assessed missionaries so that they might share the gospel well.

Nor did Calvin simply educate church planters and send them back. He wanted to remain intimately involved in the work of the gospel back in his homeland. They were more than just memories to him. They were more than just images on his fridge door, as it were. We have records of his correspondence with hundreds of church planters in which he gives them pastoral and practical advice on the establishment of underground churches.

It was profoundly effective. In 1555 there were just five underground Protestant churches in France. Four years later in 1559 that number had grown to more than one hundred. By 1562, a further three years later, it was estimated that there were over 2,000 churches in France preaching the gospel with an excess of one million people in attendance. Calvin did not just plant churches. He planted mega-churches that in turn planted more churches! True church history is a history of church planting. Calvin said:

> Seeing that God has given us such a treasure and so inestimable
> a thing as his word we must employ ourselves to it as much as

we can that it may be kept safe and sound and not perish. And let every man be sure to lock it securely in his own heart. But it is not enough to have an eye for his own salvation, but the knowledge of God must shine generally through the whole world.[2]

The New Jerusalem

We could have looked at many moments in church history. We could have looked at the Baptists in the seventeenth century. We could have looked at the Methodists in the eighteenth century. About 30 per cent of the population in England were Methodists by the end of John Wesley's life. We could have looked at the ministry of Charles H. Spurgeon in the nineteenth century. Spurgeon not only created one of the first mega-churches in the world, he also trained and commissioned church planters to plant churches around London. We could have gone to India, Germany, Russia, China to see hundreds of church-planting movements. Every church exists because by one way or another, by hook or by crook, by fair means or foul, it was planted as a church.

But church planting is not simply an historical fact. It is biblically mandated and a theological necessity. The gospel impels us to plant churches. God's purpose has always been, from the beginning, from back in eternity, to have a people for Himself, a people to whom He reveals His glory and a people in whom He displays His glory. The multiplication of churches is the necessary and inevitable outcome of this great

2. John Calvin, Sermon on 1 Timothy 2:3. Cited in *Reformed Quarterly* (Fall 2001), p. 9.

divine purpose. As it was in Antioch and Geneva, so it has been throughout history.

Church planting is not a fad. It is not an act of desperation because our numbers are dwindling. Way back in Eden God planted a church. Adam and Eve were His core team. In Matthew 5 when Jesus was on the mountain and gathered His disciples to Him He was planting a church. He was gathering His core team and embarking upon a project to plant churches throughout the world.

Our final moment, however, is taken not from history, but from the future beyond history. The whole narrative of the Bible and human history is leading to the point described in Revelation 21-22. From the beginning God has had this end in view. God started something that He intended to end in this New Creation.

In the book of Revelation John talks about Babylon and Jerusalem. He talks about the community of the beast, the community that brings great misery upon the Christian believers. This community is depicted both as a city, the city of Babylon, and as a woman, the great whore Babylon. John also talks about another community, the true community of God's people. This community is also depicted as a city and a woman. She is the new Jerusalem and the bride of the Lamb. And in the end the Bride replaces the great Prostitute.

In Revelation 21:1-2 John describes:

- 'a new heaven and a new earth'

- 'the holy city, new Jerusalem'

- 'a bride adorned for her husband'

They refer to the same entity, looked at in different ways and titled with different names. They are the bride of Christ, the Church, the gathered community of the redeemed. So the new creation is Jerusalem, which is the bride, which is the Church. In other words, the new creation is the Church of the end times.

This means the Church is not incidental, tangential or irrelevant to God's purposes. The Church is the end of history. It is what God is about. So if we provoke, incite, appeal, cajole, brow-beat people to plant churches, it is because we want people to get on board with what God is doing. Church planting is a noble endeavour and God invites us by virtue of our salvation, by virtue of our election, by virtue of our regeneration, to be involved in it – every man, every woman and every church.

Your role in the planting of churches may be different from that of other people. There is not a one-size-fits-all role of church planter. There is no magic pill for church planting, no silver bullet. But we do have the promise of Jesus that He will build His church. The case for church planting does not derive from a verse here and a verse there. It is integral to the whole sweep of the Bible from Genesis 1 to Revelation 22. This is what God is about. God is extending Himself and expending Himself in the pursuit of the church. This is why Jesus died, rose and ascended. This is why Jesus is returning. And this is the vision in which we have been invited to participate.

And as we do this, that great, prophetic hope will be fulfilled: 'The earth will be filled with the knowledge of the glory of the LORD as the waters cover the sea.' (Hab. 2:14)

4

Motive: Grace-filled church planting

MATT CHANDLER

For the love of Christ controls us, because we have concluded this: that one has died for all, therefore all have died; and he died for all, that those who live might no longer live for themselves but for him who for their sake died and was raised.

From now on, therefore, we regard no one according to the flesh. Even though we once regarded Christ according to the flesh, we regard him thus no longer. Therefore, if anyone is in Christ, he is a new creation. The old has passed away; behold, the new has come. All this is from God, who through Christ reconciled us to himself and gave us the ministry of reconciliation; that is, in Christ God was reconciling the world to himself, not counting their trespasses against them, and entrusting to us the message of reconciliation. Therefore, we are ambassadors for Christ, God making his appeal through us. We implore you on behalf of Christ, be reconciled to God. For our sake he made him to be sin who knew no sin, so that in him we might become the righteousness of God. (2 Cor. 5:14-21)

Church planting is becoming trendy. There was a time when it was what the weirdos did on the fringes of evangelicalism. It was the province of misfits and malcontents who wanted to do something different. But increasingly church planting is becoming mainstream. Now the church-planting world is populated by cool dudes. In many ways this is a hugely encouraging development. But it comes with certain dangers. Church planting has become a way to make a name or build a kingdom for yourself.

So any consideration of church planting must include a consideration of motivation because motivation matters.

Motives matter because right motives matter to God

Motivation matters for two reasons. First and primarily it matters because the Bible says it matters. It is not just the action that matters. God is concerned with what motivates the action. We see this repeatedly throughout the Scriptures. Let me give three examples.

Proverbs 21:2 says: 'Every way of a man is right in his own eyes, but the LORD weighs the heart.' We may view what we do as right. But God looks at the motives of our heart.

About five years ago I was diagnosed with a terminal form of brain cancer. I was given just two or three years to live. That was five years ago so clearly the doctors were wrong! Being told I had just a couple of years to live made me start to get my house in order. And this is what I discovered about my heart. Feel free to judge me as I write this, but know that the Lord will judge you for judging me!

With a great deal of confidence I can say that I found that I deeply and desperately love Jesus Christ. I know that is in my heart. I know that I am for Him and want to make much of His name. I know that I desire men and women to worship Him and delight in Him as my heart does.

But what I have also discovered is that, when I make much of Jesus, people make much of me. Because I love Jesus I want to make much of Him. But when I make much of Jesus, people applaud me and say, 'Man, that guy's bold; that guy's awesome.'

I found myself full of mixed motives. So I praise God for His grace. And I ask Him to continue to tease over my motives so that they will be simple and undivided. I find in this proverb the push and pull that I find in my own heart. I see here my own heart. I have to wrestle with the Lord, to lay my life before Him, and ask for an on-going process in which I become lesser and He becomes more.

Or consider Matthew 6:1: 'Beware of practising your righteousness before other people in order to be seen by them, for then you will have no reward from your Father who is in heaven.'

Clearly Jesus thinks motivation matters. It matters so much that we need to beware practising our righteousness. Now we would all agree that it is a good thing to practise righteousness. No one is going to say they are against righteousness. We know we are to pursue righteousness and walk in righteousness. But Jesus says your motivation for walking in righteousness matters. If you are walking in righteousness to be applauded or approved by others it is a false, weak righteousness. You will receive your reward in the praise of people. But you will have no reward from your Father in heaven.

Finally consider 2 Corinthians 9:7: 'Each one must give as he has decided in his heart, not reluctantly or under compulsion, for God loves a cheerful giver.'

The Lord loves the *motive* of the giver not just the *gift* of the giver. So I should be generous with great cheer. It should be my joy to give. It is not enough to do what the Lord says. There is no room for an attitude that measures out my giving, that hands over 10 per cent so I can be obedient to the letter of the law. No, I am to love being open-handed with the things with which the Lord has blessed me. Motives matter.

So the first reason you need to review your motives for church planting is because the Bible says motives matter. That is the primary reason.

Motives matter because right motives endure

But there is a second reason motives matter which is that motivations which are not anchored in the deep soil of God's word are *fickle* motivations. They will not sustain us through difficult days.

We know this to be true simply by observing our own lives and the rhythms of our culture. One of the things that happens in January every year is gyms are flooded with new members. Every January you show up in the gym and you cannot find a spot to work out. But by March all of these new people have stopped coming and the attenders at the gym return to those of you who are consistent throughout the year. New Year came and people were motivated to be healthier. They wanted to get back in shape. So they got into fitness. But then they fade. The motivation was too weak and gave way under the pressure of everyday life.

It is the same for Christians. Many of us have been motivated in spurts to memorise Scripture or to faithfully budget so we can be generous. But we have not really been motivated over the long haul of difficult days, difficult years, difficult decades.

This is important for the issue of church planting. Church planting in many parts of the world, regions like Europe, is a difficult task. The air is acidic. The ground is hard. It is true that the Holy Spirit could pour Himself out so that revival can break forth in a way most of us right now are not even imagining or dreaming is possible. But for now for most of us, the gains are slow. On top of that, much of what I see on the internet celebrates men on the fringes of orthodoxy who are experiencing a type of growth that is not normative for most of us. It is disheartening. In this kind of environment the best anchor for our motivation is the solid ground of the word of God.

So what is our motivation in planting churches that plant churches? Our goal is not to just plant a church, but rather to plant a church which has in its DNA a desire from the beginning to multiply new churches out of itself. So our goal is not a church *planted* but a church *planting* – a church planting more churches. But what is our motivation? It is an important question because if our motivation is wrong then we will lose heart and run out of steam.

The love of Christ compels us

2 Corinthians 5:14 says: 'For the love of Christ controls us.' The ESV says God's love 'controls' us while the NIV translates it as 'compels' us. The love of Christ is the fuel by which Paul is operating when he plants churches that will plant churches all over the ancient world.

We can talk about tough ground. But Paul's ground was almost certainly tougher than the one in which you are involved. Unless you have been dragged to the fringes of the city and stoned, Paul wins. Unless people have plotted to kill you, Paul wins. It is not that your context is not difficult. But *all* of Paul's contexts were difficult. Even when planting churches went well for Paul, it went badly! Even when the Holy Spirit poured Himself out in profound ways, there was a group that came right behind him to infiltrate the new church in an attempt to dismantle Paul's work. What stops Paul losing heart?

In Ephesus, for example, there was a beautiful outpouring of the Holy Spirit. But what does Paul say when he says farewell to the elders of the Ephesian church? 'Fierce wolves will come in among you, not sparing the flock.' (Acts 20:29) He is referring to the elders to whom he is talking. Some of *them* would be part of the wolves that devour this congregation. Imagine looking at a group of men into whose lives you have poured yourself. And you have been told by the Holy Spirit that these very men will tear down what you have worked so hard to build with blood, sweat and tears. That is a tough day! What keeps you going at moments like that?

The answer is that what compels Paul, what drives him, what keeps him moving, is *Christ*.

A new view of ourselves

We are right to marvel at justification. But in my experience of talking with people across the world most of us do not have a problem believing that God forgives us. But most of us struggle deeply with the idea that God might actually *like* us. We do not have a problem that we find forgiveness in the cross of Jesus Christ. But most of us lack the fuel that comes from knowing that God delights in us, that we are adopted as sons and daughters, that He loves us. That is powerful fuel. You need to get out of your head the idea that God loves a future, better, more sanctified version of you – the you that you are going to be ten years from now. Instead you need to allow the Holy Spirit to drill into your heart the idea that it is you today, blood-bought by Christ, that pleases the Lord. What motivation would stream in your heart if we could really grasp that God is for us and not against us. That would enable us to serve the Lord in difficult days.

I have often marvelled at the Apostle Paul's words in Galatians 1:16 when he says God 'was pleased to reveal his Son to me'. Whatever your background may be, it is unlikely to compare with that of Paul. He has just described his 'former life in Judaism' in which he 'persecuted the church of God violently and tried to destroy it' (Gal. 1:13). In 1 Timothy 1:16

he describes himself as 'the chief of sinners'. One morning Saul of Tarsus saddled his horse with legal documents so that he might persecute 'the Way' in Damascus. But the Lord was pleased on that day to transform Saul of Tarsus into the Apostle Paul.

To understand what it means to be sons and daughters of God is a powerful motivating force. It will motivate us regardless of the outcome of that service. For it is rooted in the love *of* Christ and a love *for* Christ – and not in our performance.

You are not the point

Paul makes this explicit as he continues in 2 Corinthians 5:14-16: 'For the love of Christ controls us, because we have concluded this: that one has died for all, therefore all have died; and he died for all, that those who live might no longer live for themselves but for him who for their sake died and was raised. From now on, therefore, we regard no one according to the flesh.'

God's love allows us to die to ourselves so that we no longer live for ourselves. When you rightly understand the forgiveness of God made available in justification and the delight of God that is brought forth in adoption, it lets you just die to yourself. It helps you understand that *you are not the point.* If you miss God's forgiving work in justification or if you miss God's adopting work in Jesus Christ then all of a sudden you are back in the mix. You matter because you are trying to justify yourself or win God's approval. It becomes all about you and your need for acceptance. It is all too possible to aim to cultivate an emphasis on grace in the ethos of your church plant in an attempt to prove yourself to others. Or it is possible to preach justification while looking to the numbers in the congregation or their response to your message to feel good about yourself.

But, when you grasp the love of Christ, you grasp the acceptance that is ours in Christ. You have died with Christ and that means you are not the point. You are not the point of your ministry. Your ministry is not the point. God's future does not depend on you. He has not put the kingdom in your hands as though all His hope lies in your ability to perform. In fact, as believers convinced of God's love for us, we should be the most free. As recipients of grace, rescued by the love of God, we are compelled simply by love.

In summary: the motivation to be churches that plant churches is simply the gospel itself. We can create all sorts of goals and taglines. But what compels us is the gospel.

The gospel changes how we view ourselves. We see in the gospel that God the Father delights in us through Christ. We therefore recognise that establishing our righteousness or winning God's approval is not the point of our ministries.

A new view of the lost

But the gospel also changes how we view other people. In 2 Corinthians 5 Paul continues: 'From now on, therefore, we regard no one according to the flesh. Even though we once regarded Christ according to the flesh, we regard him thus no longer.' (2 Cor. 5:16) We no longer see people the way we used to see people and we no longer see Christ the way we used to see Christ.

Our engagement with people radically changes. We are no longer dominated by fear because the love of Christ compels us. It is no longer about us. So the driving desire to be cool or understood or 'with it' has died also. We become free to say with the Apostle Paul, 'We are fools for Christ's sake' (1 Cor. 4:10). We no longer need the applause of men, either in the church or outside it. We no longer plant churches to make a name for ourselves or build our own kingdom. We plant churches because we want the lost to experience the love of Christ.

The gospel creates empathy in our souls towards those who are lost. Do not ever be surprised that lost people behave as unregenerate, lost people! The world is dark. We shake our fist against that darkness. We lament it. We pray for the love of Christ to transform it. But always remember that you too once walked in the domain of darkness. By His grace God has transferred us out of that kingdom and into the kingdom of His beloved Son. So we no longer regard those who are in the flesh as we once did. Now we view them with the compelling love of Christ.

We have new eyes to see them as people who can be saved by the grace of God. We understand that no-one is beyond the saving work of Jesus Christ. There are no hard places for the Lord. He knows nothing of closed countries, nor anything of revival-resistant regions. The Lord has never been shocked or perplexed, wondering what he is going to do about Europe or any other region of the world. Our Father in heaven has not lost control of Europe. His plans are His plans, and He is at work saving His people. Right now today they are out there, those who are blood-bought, those who will come to know Him.

A new creation

Paul continues in 2 Corinthians 5:17: 'Therefore, if anyone is in Christ, he is a new creation. The old has passed away; behold, the new has come.' Again Paul reminds us what it means to be united with Christ. Those who are in Christ are a new creation. Again we are reminded that a strong sense of being in Christ, delighting in Him, is imperative if we are to have the right motivation for planting churches that plant churches. It liberates you from your past.

This will hit us in different ways at different times. Several years ago I was speaking at an Acts 29 pastors' conference in Houston, Texas. We were meeting about forty-five minutes from where I used to live. So during a break, I drove down to my home town because I wanted to take some pictures of my old house. I wanted to be able to show my children where their father grew up. As I drove into town I passed a field in which I got into a fist fight with a kid when I was in high school. I humiliated him to the extent that, unless Christ has done a great work in his life, I suspect my name would still churn up his heart in rage. Then I passed a house where I had been involved in things at a party that are too wicked to name. I passed another house where I was a part of some of the most shameful things I have ever done. Everything in that town reminded me of my rebellion against the Lord. Driving back to the conference I felt almost nauseous in my gut at the shame in my heart. I began to feel condemned. Ironically I was on my way back to preach on 'a pastors' need for the gospel'. But first I had to preach that message to myself. On the drive back up I was reminded of this fact: That Matt Chandler is dead!

That rebellious kid is dead. The Matt Chandler driving this car now lives 'by faith in the Son of God, who loved me and gave himself for me' (Gal. 2:20).

So it is not about my past. My past has been redeemed. The idea of being made new in Christ sets us free to wrestle well with the accusations of the Enemy and to wrestle well with the game of comparison with other people. To understand that you are new in Christ allows your identity to be formed in Him. It enables you to combat thoughts like, I wish I could have that; I wish I was better at that; I wish I had that result; I wish I could make that happen. It lets you just die to all of that and say instead, 'Thank you, Lord.'

The ministry of reconciliation

And look what happens when our identity is formed in Christ: 'All this is from God who in Christ reconciled us to himself and gave us the ministry of reconciliation.' (2 Cor. 5:18)

Christ has reconciled us to Himself *and* He has given to us the very ministry that we were the recipients of when we were reconciled. 'That is, in Christ God was reconciling the world to himself, not counting their trespasses against them.' (2 Cor. 5:19) God has reconciled us to Himself through Christ, forgiving our sins. But Paul goes on to say that God is also 'entrusting to us the message of reconciliation'. Not only have we been reconciled, but we have also been given the ministry of reconciliation.

Church planting is a ministry of reconciliation. We proclaim the message that God is no longer holding the trespasses of the world against those who will repent and put their faith in Christ. We have been entrusted with this message of good news. We are gathering people reconciled to God by the gospel into a community of reconciliation.

'We are ambassadors for Christ,' says verse 20. Do we live in a way that mirrors well the righteousness found in God in Christ? We are to be a people of joy, people who walk in trust rather than fear. In our church plants people should see gladness instead of despair, discipline instead of chaos, and joy instead of happiness. Happiness is fragile. It easily breaks. It is not sustaining. That is because happiness is dictated by our circumstances. We are happy when things are going as we want them to go. But Christians are to be people not of happiness but of joy. Joy is a gladness in God that our circumstances cannot affect. It remains steadfast regardless of the current events in our lives. We are ambassadors and that shapes how we live.

But we have also been entrusted with 'the *message* of reconciliation'. It is not just our lives, but also our mouths that must herald the good news of the reconciling work of Jesus Christ.

What are your motives?

What is it that drives us? What is the anchor for the church planter and his team? It is the gospel. For all other motivations will fail you. The difficulty of the work, the sinfulness of your own heart, the desire to be applauded and the longing to be seen as a success are all powerful forces. They will chisel away at us. We may start finding our worth by how many people show up each Sunday. We may begin to expect a type of entitlement that God considers offensive rather than the humility that understands that we are the servants of all.

So a key question you need to process in your own heart is this: What are your motives? Whether you are investigating church planting or already moving towards planting or an existing church that wants to get into planting, you need to ask what it is that is really driving that desire. We need to wrestle when we see things that are inconsistent with a gospel motivation. We must confess and repent of them.

This will require a type of humility among the leaders of leaders that I have found to be rare. For it is in our weaknesses that the gospel is often seen most clearly.

Some time ago I received an unhelpful, negative email. I knew the Bible says I should respond with gentleness. So I typed up a kind and gracious response, and then copied in the elders of my church. Later Brian Miller, our lead pastor and chairman of our elder board, came to my office and said: 'I'm so proud of you, Matt. I think that type of godliness is rare. I so appreciate it.' In that moment I could have puffed up and thanked him. I could have pretended that I had sought the Lord in prayer and felt that what this brother needed was compassion. But that would have made me a liar. It would have represented a false kind of strength that is built on me and not Christ. So instead, by the grace of God, I took the opportunity to confess my sinful attitudes. Together Brian and I prayed for heart change. It was an opportunity for me to build my foundation again on Christ instead of trying to build it on me. We must get over ourselves! As John the Baptist said: 'He must increase, but I must decrease' (John 3:30).

You need to do the work of evaluating the motives of your heart for they will spring up often and surprise you. Do not be surprised by your surprise. Be willing and diligent to do the hard work of confession and repentance. You are not above it. When Luther said that all of life is repentance he meant that there will be an on-going discipline in your life of confession and repentance. It means there will never be a day for you when you are not in need of saying, 'Oh, I have done it again. Help me, Lord.'

And if you can anchor your heart in the gospel, then if it takes you thirty years to grow a church of three people you might walk in *holy* discontent, but you will not walk in *sinful* discontent. I think we are going to be surprised in heaven at who is well rewarded and who is not. That is because the Lord sees the heart. He knows our faithfulness. He does not celebrate bigness over smallness. He is the God who said: 'Gideon, if I let you beat that army you're going to get big-headed. So I'm going to cut down your army.' 'It's still too big. Cut it down further. You need to know it's just me who wins the battle.' This seems to be the habit of the Lord – paring down and then working for the glory of *His* name.

So may your motives be as pure as possible. And may you be quick to repent when they are not.

5

Method: Word-centred church planting

REUBEN HUNTER

The *'For Dummies'* range of books has become a phenomenal success. Taking, as they do, the complexities of anything from computer programming to French wine, and simplifying them for the everyman, the sales of these books have exploded. The reason for this success is undoubtedly because the authors have tapped into our desire to be given a simple way to master something that, otherwise, might take a long time. They offer a shortcut to success.

It should come as no surprise that when it comes to church planting there are plenty of 'For Dummies' guides available. Christian publishers have missed the boat if they haven't got their version of 'Five Easy Steps to Successful Church Planting' complete with a foreword by their successful planter of choice. On the whole this is a good thing and we need all the help we can get. But the danger with many of them is that pragmatism and personal testimony win out over biblical teaching. Any church we want to see planted, if it is to be what God has designed it to be, must be established according to Scripture.

Allied to my desire to be biblical is also a desire to be contextual. Just as Scripture presents different approaches to church planting in different contexts, so I want to recognise that we work in different contexts with different backgrounds and different cultures. This means any talk of church-planting methodology, if it is to be biblical, must be able to accommodate this contextual breadth. There can be no 'one-size-fits-all' church-planting method. So what are we going to do?

We need to start by stepping back from *particulars* to look at *principles*. And the Apostle Paul helps us with this perhaps most clearly in 1 Thessalonians 2. Here he speaks clearly about his own church-planting method when he went to Thessalonica.

Acts 17 tells the story of Paul's church planting in this city. As was his habit, the Apostle went first to the synagogue and reasoned with the Jews that Jesus was the Christ. He also interacted with the god-fearing Greeks who worshipped at the synagogue, but who were not full converts to Judaism.

He called on them to recognise that Jesus was in fact the King, not Caesar. From both these groups, the Jews and the Greeks, this new church was formed. But not long after Paul's arrival, unbelieving Jews stirred up a riot, a riot that ended with Paul and Silas having to leave this young church. They had to flee under the cover of darkness in fear of their lives.

Because of the short time that Paul spent in Thessalonica and because of the hasty nature of his exit, it seems that opponents had come in. These opponents had begun to unsettle this young church, casting doubts over Paul and his credibility. Was Paul a fake? After all, he did not stay long and he left in a hurry. Was he just another one of these professional speakers who breezes through town, telling people what they want to hear and taking their money?

Paul has heard of these accusations. And so he writes to tell this young church that they were not deceived. He is a legitimate Apostle and so in 1 Thessalonians 2 he provides an *apologia* for his ministry:

> For you yourselves know, brothers, that our coming to you was not in vain. But though we had already suffered and been shamefully treated at Philippi, as you know, we had boldness in our God to declare to you the gospel of God in the midst of much conflict. For our appeal does not spring from error or impurity or any attempt to deceive, but just as we have been approved by God to be entrusted with the gospel, so we speak, not to please man, but to please God who tests our hearts. For we never came with words of flattery, as you know, nor with a pretext for greed – God is witness. Nor did we seek glory from

people, whether from you or from others, though we could have made demands as apostles of Christ. But we were gentle among you, like a nursing mother taking care of her own children. So, being affectionately desirous of you, we were ready to share with you not only the gospel of God but also our own selves, because you had become very dear to us.

For you remember, brothers, our labour and toil: we worked night and day, that we might not be a burden to any of you, while we proclaimed to you the gospel of God. You are witnesses, and God also, how holy and righteous and blameless was our conduct towards you believers. For you know how, like a father with his children, we exhorted each one of you and encouraged you and charged you to walk in a manner worthy of God, who calls you into his own kingdom and glory.

And we also thank God constantly for this, that when you received the word of God, which you heard from us, you accepted it not as the word of men but as what it really is, the word of God, which is at work in you believers. For you, brothers, became imitators of the churches of God in Christ Jesus that are in Judea. For you suffered the same things from your own countrymen as they did from the Jews, who killed both the Lord Jesus and the prophets, and drove us out, and displease God and oppose all mankind by hindering us from speaking to the Gentiles that they might be saved – so as always to fill up the measure of their sins. But God's wrath has come upon them at last!

But since we were torn away from you, brothers, for a short time, in person not in heart, we endeavoured the more eagerly and with great desire to see you face to face, because we wanted to come to you – I, Paul, again and again – but Satan hindered us. For what is our hope or joy or crown of boasting before our

Lord Jesus at his coming? Is it not you? For you are our glory and joy. (1 Thess. 2:1-20)

What we have here is Paul the church planter telling us what he did as he sought to plant this church. This is Paul's church-planting method, if you will. Now, although Paul is an Apostle and that creates some distance from us, I want us to work through his argument highlighting four principles as we go. Each principle runs all the way through the chapter and while they apply broadly to all pastoral ministry, they apply particularly to church planting.

So there are many things that you *may* do as you plant a church. But here are four things that you *must* do.

1. Lead with God's word

A simple glance at Paul's ministry reveals that the proclamation of God's word was right at the centre of all that he did. And Thessalonica was no different.

- 'We had boldness in our God to declare to you the gospel of God.' (v. 2)

- 'We have been approved by God to be entrusted with the gospel, so we speak, not to please man, but to please God who tests our hearts.' (v. 4)

- 'We were ready to share with you not only the gospel of God …' (v. 8)

- 'We proclaimed to you the gospel of God.' (v. 9)

- '… the word of God, which you heard from us, you accepted it not as the word of men but as what it really

is, the word of God, which is at work in you believers.'
(v. 13)

- '... by hindering us from speaking to the Gentiles that they might be saved.' (v. 16)

Paul's ministry is first and foremost a ministry of God's word. The reason for this is simple: the presence and the work of God in the world is mediated to us by His word. Throughout the Bible, from start to finish, God's word creates, sustains, gives life, sanctifies. God's word brings light, powerfully pushing back darkness in the world. This is why Paul prioritised God's word in his ministry. This is why when he passes on the baton of ministry to Timothy he urged him to prioritise the proclamation of the word. 'Until I come, devote yourself to the public reading of Scripture, to exhortation, to teaching.' (1 Tim. 4:13) 'I charge you in the presence of God and of Christ Jesus, who is to judge the living and the dead, and by his appearing and his kingdom: preach the word; be ready in season and out of season; reprove, rebuke, and exhort, with complete patience and teaching.' (2 Tim. 4:1-2) And this is where we must start in our church planting today.

I recognise that this statement is not a great revelation to evangelicals. But it is important to remind ourselves of the priority of the word in order that our practice on the ground reflects this reality. Whatever you are doing, without God's word your new church has nothing distinctive to offer the community into which you plant. It offers nothing that any other organisation could not provide to some degree. Indeed you will not actually have a church. With the right gifts, skills and charisma you might be able to gather together a community of reasonably caring people. You might be able to help people with emotional and social problems. You might even be able to mobilise a group of people to do helpful things that serve the community in which you operate. But you will not have a church. In his book on the church Edmund Clowney says: 'The church is the community of the word, the word that reveals the plan and purpose of God.'[1]

So we need to be careful that we do not simply affirm a commitment to God's word in a statement of faith, without working hard on the ground to have it at the very heart of our church's life. It needs to be shaping all the decisions that we make and driving all that we do.

We also need to take care not to assume the centrality of God's word, but functionally prioritise other things – even good and important things – because we err if we allow anything to depose the word of God from its central place. Clowney again:

> In every task of the church the ministry of the word of God is central. It is the word that calls us to worship, addresses us in worship, teaches us how to worship, and enables us to praise God and to encourage one another. By the word we are given life and nurtured to maturity in Christ. The word is the sword of the Spirit to correct us and the bread of the Spirit to feed us. In the mission of the church it is the word of God that calls the nations to the Lord. In the teaching of the word we make disciples of the nations. The growth of the church is the growth of the word.

---

1. Edmund Clowney, *The Church* (IVP, 1995), p. 16.

Where there is a famine of the word no expertise in business administration or group dynamics will build Christ's church.[2]

Keeping the Bible at the centre of our churches is vital, and in practice this takes three things.

First, it takes *discipline*. When you start, particularly if you are planting a church from scratch, if something is going to get done, then the chances are that you are the person who is going to have to do it. And there are hundreds of things that you could do – fundraising, meeting people, developing a website, updating social media, formulating a Sunday school curriculum, providing coffee and tea after the service, organising your signage, advertising your presence. They are all important things. But on your priority list they need to find their place underneath your careful study and preaching of Scripture. To prioritise God's word like this – which involves saying 'no' to doing good things – takes discipline.

Second, it takes *humility*. There are lots of things to which you could give your time when planting a church that will get you a pat on the back. There are some things you could do that will make you look good. But few people will praise you for teaching the Bible. Building the church on God's word is not glamorous, and it takes attention away from us. That is a good thing, but it does take humility.

Third, it takes *faith*. The Lord Jesus Christ has promised that He will build His church. That is a promise that we have to receive by faith. This is particularly the case in regions like Europe in these days where the life-giving and sanctifying work

---

2. Clowney, *The Church*, pp. 199-200.

of the word of God is painstakingly slow. So to keep His word at the heart of your ministry requires you to trust Him. All ministry requires this sort of trust, and you might think that point is obvious, but in the day to day of planting a new church it is tempting to think that other things are more important than time in the study. Keeping the Bible central takes faith.

Do you believe that the one thing that your neighbourhood and your people need is the word of God? It really is! So, as Mike McKinley has put it: 'Teach God's word. Evangelise using God's word. Disciple people using God's word. And then, when you launch a public service, preach God's word.'[3]

I also want to urge you not to lose your nerve on the sermon. In a right desire to recover the importance of word ministry in other contexts in church life, I think in recent times there has been a shift away from authoritative preaching. This is a mistake. Unsurprisingly, preaching is what Paul had in mind when he instructs Timothy to 'preach the word' and it has been the practice of the church down the ages. God's design is that His people gather to humbly listen to a man who stands in His place, to deliver His message, and through that event His Spirit works in power to bring His chosen purposes to pass.

2. Lead with integrity

The context for Paul's ministry, both prior to coming to Thessalonica when he was in Philippi and in Thessalonica itself, was one of great suffering and opposition. So it becomes abundantly clear that Paul was not in ministry for himself. In

---

3. Mike McKinley, *Church Planting is for Wimps* (Crossway, 2010), p. 53.

verse 2 he says: 'But though we had already suffered and been shamefully treated at Philippi, as you know, we had boldness in our God to declare to you the gospel of God in the midst of much conflict.'

A willingness to suffer is an essential mark of any authentic gospel minister. Suffering is not a sign of failure. In verse 1 Paul says: 'For you yourselves know, brothers, that our coming to you was not in vain.' Suffering is, instead, a sign that a ministry is cross-shaped after the pattern of our Master.

Nevertheless suffering will test your integrity like little else. While you might not experience what Paul did, you will be amazed at the frustrations, the pressures and the temptations that come your way when you set out to plant a new church.

But look at how Paul, in the face of his opponents, positively points to his integrity. In verses 3-4 he says: 'For our appeal does not spring from error or impurity or any attempt to deceive, but just as we have been approved by God to be entrusted with the gospel, so we speak, not to please man, but to please God who tests our hearts.'

Paul does not tamper with his message. His appeal is gospel truth not error. He is not driven by pride or popularity. His motives are pure rather than impure. His behaviour was above board. He was transparent, holy, righteous, blameless, without deceit. And he can call God as his witness to verify these claims: 'You are witnesses, and God also, how holy and righteous and blameless was our conduct towards you believers.' (1 Thess. 2:10)

We should long for this transparency in our lives and in our ministries, especially in the hothouse of church planting. It's sometimes said that when you're church planting it can feel like your life has been plugged into an amplifier. In this kind of situation integrity and transparency are particularly important. Your life and your views are constantly scrutinised, and it's not just your theological views. I have been asked about my views on everything from politics to who I think will win particular sports tournaments. You are scrutinised because, if Christians are going to follow you into this crazy project, they need to know they can trust you. They need to know they can follow you. They need to be sure it is not going to end badly.

But it's not just the Christians who will be scrutinising you. Unbelievers that you connect with in your area, or those who come along to your church, are also watching you like a hawk. The idea of starting a new church is outside every category a secular person has and they want to know what on earth is going on. And, sadly, in Europe in these days unbelievers are expecting to see something unscrupulous going on. The church has a bad reputation so people are looking for a chink in your public image, for some hypocrisy, for gaps where life and lip do not match. If we do not have integrity we will be found out in no time.

It is all very well saying that we should lead with integrity. But how do we do this? Key for Paul is his mind-set. Paul's mind-set was to please God above everything else and the same is to be true of us in every area of our life. Our *manner* is the fruit of our *mind-set*.

So ask yourself the question: What is your motivation for planting a church? As we saw in chapter four, it is to be the gospel. And in our better moments we really do want it to be the gospel and the glory of the Lord Jesus Christ. But, if we're honest, when we peel back the layers of our heart, we see other motives at play. In some contexts it may be money. Even in contexts where ministers are not well paid, it is possible to be greedy and to use your leadership as cover for this. It may be a desire for control. Or maybe you think of yourself as the person who has the solution to all that is broken in the traditional church.

None of our motives are entirely pure in anything that we do. And if we wait around for our motives to be perfect then no churches would be planted. But you need to be sure that your mind-set is committed to pleasing God, for it is God who tests our hearts.

Practically speaking, if you are not committed to pleasing God then you will be a puppet to the opinions of others. And when this is the case you are vulnerable to all kinds of things, from tweaking your teaching to suit your hearers, to misrepresenting the shape your ministry will take to appeal to potential donors. The wealthy man who shares few, if any, of your core convictions but likes the idea of helping 'the church' needs to know that a large part of your week will be spent studying the Scriptures. You will only be up front about that if your heart's desire is to please God above all.

Try to create as much distance between you and the bank account as possible. That is not always easy when you are getting started, particularly if you are the main fundraiser. But as soon as you can, try to get a third party involved to provide as much transparency as possible. Don't allow the way money is handled in your new church plant to threaten your integrity.

Of course, another possible pitfall is the motivation of your own reputation. When I started out I was astonished at the number of people – leaders, friends, godly people, theologically like-minded people, people who talked and practised church planting and were for church planting – who when I talked about our plans looked at me with a face that said: 'Why on earth would you do that?' or flatly told me it was a bad idea.

When we talked about our planting plans, my wife and I said from the start that we would embark on the whole project trusting the Lord. We were full of faith and trust in God's power and sovereign purposes. But I can tell you that after I had endured the umpteenth patronising or negative conversation, I felt a huge motivation to make things work and to prove those people wrong! But that is no motivation to plant a church. When your pride is the motivator then your mind-set is wrong and your integrity is shot.

Let me assure you, if your identity hangs on the success (or failure) of your church-planting endeavour, then you will die. Make a will and tell your loved ones, because it will happen. None of us want that so please choose the alternative: pursue a God-centred mind-set so that you can lead with integrity.

3. Lead with love

Paul was an apostle. So by rights he could have insisted on certain things when he was with the Thessalonians. He could have asserted his authority, dishing out orders, even demanding financial support. But instead he chose none of that. Instead he employs two striking images – he likens his approach to that of loving parents.

Be like a mother

First, Paul likens himself to a mother. In verses 6-9 he says:

> Nor did we seek glory from people, whether from you or from others, though we could have made demands as apostles of Christ. But we were gentle among you, like a nursing mother taking care of her own children. So, being affectionately desirous of you, we were ready to share with you not only the gospel of God but also our own selves, because you had become very dear to us. For you remember, brothers, our labour and toil: we worked night and day, that we might not be a burden to any of you, while we proclaimed to you the gospel of God.

Paul says he was 'gentle among you, like a nursing mother'. Think of the tenderness and care a mother takes over her new-born child. I have been reminded again of the force of this imagery with the recent arrival of our daughter Martha. My wife is ceaseless in her care for this little one, and everything is done with great care and tenderness. She gives and gives and gives again to provide for Martha's needs and help her flourish.

Paul was like this among the Thessalonians. He could have milked this church, but instead he gave of himself in order to provide the 'milk' of the life-giving gospel to them. In verse 9 he speaks of his 'labour and toil' and how he 'worked night and day'. Like a mother, who can't simply 'clock-off' when she wants, Paul is gently, lovingly and tirelessly committed to serving these young believers.

There is an important challenge here for many of us. Often church planters are talked about as entrepreneurs or as 'natural' or 'strong' leaders. But these can be beautiful euphemisms for being heavy-handed, harsh, tough, stubborn. This is not Paul's image of the natural or strong leader. He says: 'We were gentle among you.'

This still applies when it comes to dealing with the angular people who often seem to crop up in church-planting situations. Can you be gentle with the man who always wants to talk to you about his theological hobby-horse? Can you be gentle with the woman who is supportive to your face, but disruptive when she talks to others in the church? Or what about the person whom you seem to have nothing in common with and they just rub you the wrong way? 'Being affectionately desirous of you, we were ready to share with you not only the gospel of God but also our own selves, because you had become very dear to us.' I am certain not everyone in Thessalonica was a joy to spend time with. But Paul can still say that they were dear to him.

Are you prepared to keep on giving of yourself with that motherly devotion? To keep going when no-one thanks you for it, just like a new mum? Paul's imagery here is so profound, for babies are not great encouragers. They don't give much back in terms of appreciation! Will you give of yourself week after week, month after month, year after year?

No one gets into church planting if they want an easy life. But there are ways to spend your time that can be dressed up as ministry, but which are actually a cover for laziness. We need to be honest with ourselves and keep Paul's imagery of the loving mother at the front of our minds, an image of sacrificial love shown in affection and commitment.

Be like a father

The second image Paul employs is that of a father. In verses 10-12 he says:

> You are witnesses, and God also, how holy and righteous and blameless was our conduct towards you believers. For you know how, like a father with his children, we exhorted each one of you and encouraged you and charged you to walk in a manner worthy of God, who calls you into his own kingdom and glory.

At the end of the letter Paul prays for the Thessalonians: 'Now may the God of peace himself sanctify you completely, and may your whole spirit and soul and body be kept blameless at the coming of our Lord Jesus Christ.' (1 Thess. 5:23) What Paul wants for the Thessalonians in 5:23 is what he says in 2:10 he himself modelled to them. Like any good father he leads by example and he wants them to emulate the life he has lived in front of them. He set them an example in faith, life and purity. And then he backed that up with the encouragement and exhortation that all children need if they are to persevere in something they find hard.

We also see here that there is a destination in Paul's mind in all of this, namely, the kingdom and glory of God. He takes joy in people coming to faith and persevering to their heavenly reward.

A few years ago, on holiday on the southern Irish coast, I took my son down on to a spur of rock that juts out into the sea. I had been there before and knew it was a great spot where you can sit with your feet hanging over the crystal clear water below, looking all the way down into its depths. It was a beautiful day and I knew my son would love it. But it is a bit of climb to get there with big boulders to clamber over. For a four-year-old it was going to be hard. I knew, however, that he would enjoy the achievement of getting there and enjoy the spot once he had made it there. Along the way he got tired and started to complain. When that happened I did not say, 'OK, we're done. Let's go back.' Nor did I say, 'This is embarrassing, you're a disgrace to the family name.' No, I encouraged him. 'Look,' I said, 'let's just get up the next bit and keep going. You're going to love it when we get there.' And indeed when we ended up on the rock, he had a big smile on his face. He was delighted because he had done it and was enjoying it. And I was delighted because he was delighted.

This is the sort of thing that Paul has in mind when he talks of this fatherly love. The destination is the kingdom and the glory of God. He does not want the Thessalonians to miss out on this. So he encourages them, exhorts them, urges them to keep on pursuing godliness because he knows that when they get there they will rejoice. And there will be joy for Paul as well. For him it will be the joy of seeing those under his care finish the race and make it to glory.

Leading with love means leading by fatherly example. So there can be no, 'Do as I say, not as I do'. It means encouraging those God entrusts to your care – not bullying them, nor patronising them – but urging them towards godliness and maturity. And when they get weary, give them a vision of what lies ahead if they persevere to the end.

Paul is modelling both a *maternal* and a *paternal* love for this church. It is obvious that you cannot do this from a distance. Particularly when starting a new church, you need to open your home. You need to open your life. And you need to do that not just when it suits you. It is a costly love to which Paul is calling us.

This costly love cannot just be switched on in a moment. It is the fruit of God's Spirit. Therefore we need to ask God to give it to us. We need to wrestle in prayer, asking that He would grow in our hearts this sort of love which enables us to be this sort of leader.

Planting churches that in turn plant more churches will involve a lot of strategy and systems. But in all of this we must never forget that our ministry is fundamentally and unbendingly about people.

In the early days, when you are getting started, you are bound to think about numbers because in those early days numbers might be the difference between viability and extinction. But in this situation, too, you must remember that the people that are there are the people whom God has sent to you and your job is to lead them with love. You might wish that there were more of them. You might wish that they were more gifted or more generous. But they are never just 'bums on seats' or names on a membership directory. They are never a means to your strategic ends.

You can tell how you are doing with the 'heart-check' we find in verse 17: 'But since we were torn away from you, brothers, for a short time, in person not in heart.' Paul's language is strong. He speaks of being 'torn away'. A horrible breach has occurred. But they have never left his mind, so affectionate is he for them. Ask yourself the question: If you had to leave your church tomorrow for some reason, would it grieve you?

Sinclair Ferguson spoke a few years ago at a conference about lessons he had learned over a lifetime of pastoral ministry. He started by saying: 'Perhaps the most important thing that I've learned is the absolute centrality of loving the people God gives us to serve.'[4] He then went on: 'That's more important than anything else. That's actually more important than our gifts because our gifts without love will be like noisy cymbals and our ministry will be empty.' He adds:

> I think often for younger men that's quite a challenge. We go into ministry and we have a deep sense of the importance of truth. But the only people who will gather around you because of the importance of truth are either people who are poorly taught in Scripture or cranks. And both of them will gather around the notion that the most important thing is truth, truth without love. But in the gospel there is no such reality as truth without love. And so it's very important for us, especially if we have a real passion for preaching, to understand that what is going to oil the wheels of our preaching is that the people to whom we preach know that we actually love them.

---

4. Sinclair Ferguson, 'Best Lessons from a Lifetime of Pastoring' (3 February 2014), Desiring God, <http://www.desiringgod.org/conference-messages/best-lessons-from-a-lifetime-of-pastoring>.

4. Lead with the future in view

It is striking how the return of Christ frames both Paul's approach in the letter as a whole and informs his ministry as he talks about it here in chapter 2. We have already seen in verse 12 that the future kingdom and glory of God are to be held out as motives for godliness. But Paul returns to the theme of Christ's return both in terms of judgment and in terms of joy. In verse 16 he says that those who are hindering the proclamation of the gospel are filling 'up the measure of their sins. But God's wrath has come upon them at last!' It is literally that the wrath of God has come upon them at '*the last*', that is on the last day. They are heading for wrath. Then in verses 19-20 he speaks of joy: 'For what is our hope or joy or crown of boasting before our Lord Jesus at his coming? Is it not you? For you are our glory and joy.'

This fourth principle is the perspective that motivates the other three. One day every soul that has ever walked the earth will stand before the Lord at the judgment throne. Those who have rejected Him will spend an eternity facing His terrible wrath. But those who have received His grace by faith in His Son will receive the crown of righteousness and go to eternal joy. Some will go one way; some will go the other way. And it is knowing that this day is coming that motivates all that Paul does. The coming judgment spurs him on to share the gospel with those who do not know Christ. And the coming joy motivates him to serve the Thessalonian believers. As we have already seen, the fact that these people will be there celebrating together with him on that day is what enables him to lead in the sacrificial way he does.

We must allow the desperate future that awaits unbelievers to drive us forward in church planting. Paul's entire ministry was shaped by a desire to see men and women bow the knee to Jesus Christ. We need to ask the Lord to give us that same broken-hearted love for those who need to be reached. But also the thing that will motivate us to lead with God's word, with integrity and with love is the glorious gospel hope that one day we will stand in glory and there will be men and women standing there who are only there because, in God's strength, we were faithful. We must plant churches with that goal in view.

It's worth it

Lead with God's word. No one may thank you now for your preaching. Some of you know what it is like to stare at a Bible passage and then stare at the wall and then stare at the text again and then get up from your desk, still none the wiser. And having wrestled to get a sermon for Sunday, then Monday morning arrives and we have to do it all over again. If you know that experience then you know that it is hard to keep going. But when you see those people for whom you have done it in glory, then it will all have been worth it.

Lead with integrity. The temptation to self-protection is ever present. We shrink back from suffering. The desire to further our own reputation is ever-present. But, when the pressure is on, remind yourself of the joy that will flood your heart when you see that person in glory – that person whose faith you did not wreck because you refused to compromise or walk away. Allow the joy of seeing that person on the day of glory to motivate you. On that day you will realise that it will all have been worth it.

Lead with love. No one may know the heartbreak you feel or the tears you shed over the people in your care. You open your home and your life again and again only for people to abuse that generosity. You pour yourself out in pastoral care only to have people persist in lying to you or remain hard-hearted. If, by taking it on the chin, you see them through to glory then your labour is not in vain. Because on that day you will realise that it will all have been worth it.

There is no 'Church Planting for Dummies' because there are no short-cuts to success when we are seeking to plant the gospel into unreached communities. God builds His church in His time. But as we labour in prayer and, in the power of His Holy Spirit, embrace these four principles, we will see healthy churches planted and established even in the hardest places. May God alone get the glory.

6

Means: Spirit-empowered church planting

MATT CHANDLER

One of the privileges I enjoy in my role with Acts 29 is visiting other parts of the world. It is always healthy to be reminded of how significant the enterprise is that we have been caught up in, and to be reminded often that it is far from over. As Habakkuk tells us, the great prophetic hope is that 'the earth will be filled with the knowledge of the glory of the LORD as the waters cover the sea' (Hab. 2:14). If you have spent any time on the ocean, you will know that there is water everywhere! We have been given a task that cannot fail. That is a good thing to keep before us, especially during difficult seasons as we seek to be faithful to all God has called us to be and do for Him.

But we do also need to think about what are the primary means towards that great end. Without claiming to be exhaustive, the theme of this book is that church planting must be ranked highly among those means. A healthy and robust church that understands the gospel is a church that will be actively involved in planting other churches, which then plant more churches.

In the book of Acts we see the movement of the gospel clearly. We see it, not just in the sending out of missionaries to seek disciples, but in the formation of churches-in-context to make disciples. Luke shows us that the goal of the gospel is not simply evangelism, but disciple-making. This might be disappointing to some. The book of Acts might be the book where you expect to find out more about the Holy Spirit and associated phenomena. But it is not primarily about the gifts of the Spirit. Of course, they occur in the narrative. But Luke's purpose is not to provide a manual on spiritual gifts. His aim is to show the movement of the gospel in the formation of churches.

This raises the question that relates to all the historical material in the Bible: Is it merely descriptive or is it in some sense prescriptive? Is it simply telling us what occurred or is it telling us how life should be lived? It is a simple enough question. But the answer is not straightforward. It is clearly not entirely prescriptive. The last time your church appointed a pastor, I suspect you did not cast lots to make the decision as they do when they appoint Matthias in Acts 1. No one has ever taken that text and said, 'You know what, we need a new worship leader. Where's the dice?' The book of Acts resists such stark either-or alternatives. There are in fact elements of both description and prescription. There are things we should imitate because it is clear that the Lord will be pleased by the pursuit of such things.

But, as important as these issues and questions are, we are in danger of missing the wood for the trees. The purpose of the book of Acts is found not at Pentecost but rather in 1:8: 'But you will receive power when the Holy Spirit has come upon you, and you will be my witnesses in Jerusalem and in all Judea and Samaria, and to the end of the earth.'

In keeping with the thrust of Luke's account, we will look at *how* church planting has occurred from the day of Pentecost onwards as the gospel moves out of Jerusalem across the Roman world and across the globe. We will follow this movement of the gospel which has reached even as far as here and now, so that we are caught up in this beautiful thing called the bride of Jesus Christ.

In Acts 1 the resurrected Christ has spent forty days with His disciples. He is now about to ascend to be back with His Father, and take His rightful place as the Lord at the Father's right hand. Immediately prior to the ascension He tells His followers to wait in Jerusalem. That is because, if they are to fulfil His orders, they are going to need power from outside of themselves. He promises they will receive the necessary equipping to become His witnesses – the gift of the Holy Spirit.

The New Testament is very clear that we receive the Holy Spirit at conversion. Without Him there is no regeneration. It is the Holy Spirit who awakens us to our need, convinces us of our sin and converts us to Christ. He takes up His residence in the heart of the believer. So I am not convinced by the argument that there is a second experience that turns you from a mere novice into a member of the A-Team. But I am absolutely persuaded that the Spirit equips and empowers us for specific tasks, again and again. Churches are planted through the work of the Spirit. What happens in Acts 2 happens again at the end of Acts 4. There they pray for boldness and once again they are filled with the Holy Spirit. Notice how similar the two accounts are:

- 'And they were all filled with the Holy Spirit and began to speak in other tongues as the Spirit gave them utterance.' (2:4)

- 'And when they had prayed, the place in which they were gathered together was shaken, and they were all filled with the Holy Spirit and continued to speak the word of God with boldness.' (4:31)

So regeneration is the work of the Spirit. We receive Him at conversion when we are sealed and He begins to dwell in us. But how does this assertion fit with what Jesus did with His disciples in John 20:22: 'he breathed on them and said to them, "Receive the Holy Spirit."' If they received the Holy

Spirit at this point, why does Jesus tell them in Acts 1:4 and 8 to remain in Jerusalem until they have received the enabling power of the Spirit? He uses a different expression in Luke 24:49: 'And behold, I am sending the promise of my Father upon you. But stay in the city until you are clothed with power from on high.' What does it mean for the Holy Spirit to come upon us and for us to be clothed with power from on high?

Martyn Lloyd-Jones in his book *Joy Unspeakable* uses a helpful illustration in this regard. One does not have to share Lloyd-Jones' view of a second assurance-giving baptism of, or sealing by, the Holy Spirit to share his longing for the church to experience more Spirit-given confidence for witness. He describes this as a son walking down the street holding his father's hand. The child feels safe as they are together on a journey. According to Lloyd-Jones, this describes the normal Christian experience. But then the level of intensity rises as the father suddenly sweeps up his son, pulls him in tight, kisses his face, holds him out in front of him, looks into his eyes and says, 'I love you so much, son. I'm so glad to be your father.' This is how Lloyd-Jones expressed it:

> The child is simply stunned. He doesn't know whether to cry, or to shout or to fall down or to run he was so happy. The fuses of love are so overloaded they almost blow out. The sub-conscious doubts that he wasn't even thinking about at the time, but that do pop up every now and then, are gone and in their place is utter and indestructible assurance so that you know, that you know, that you know that God is real, that Jesus lives, that you are loved and that to be saved is the greatest thing in the world.

And when you walk down the street you can scarcely contain yourself and you want to cry out, 'My Father loves me, My Father loves me, oh what a great Father I have, what a Father, what a Father.'[1]

This is what occurs when the Holy Spirit comes upon you or when you are clothed in power from on high. There is a boldness which replaces our normal timidity. Even if you consider yourself to be a timid person, the last vestiges of nervousness vanish when the Holy Spirit clothes you. The weight of delight in God drives out any fear or concern for how you are perceived. That is what it means to be clothed with power from on high.

Jesus says to His disciples that there is power coming for them. If we are honest, the majority of our life does not look like that. In the terms of Lloyd-Jones' analogy, we spend the majority of life holding hands with our heavenly Father as if we are just walking down the street. We faithfully take God at his word, taking one step at a time, trusting that God is leading us into joy. But occasionally we get clothed in power from on high. And this makes us hungry for more. This is not a power we can control. It is not a trance to incite or an experience to summon by singing a song for the hundredth time. It is not found by taking yourself away for two days to pray and fast to receive the power from on high. Lloyd-Jones said that the Father picks his child up suddenly 'out of nowhere'.

So we can expect most of our days will be spent in the contentment of holding the Father's hand, as it were, following

---

1. Martyn Lloyd-Jones, *Joy Unspeakable* (David C. Cook, 1995), p. 105.

His lead, feeling safe as we are guided by His providence and His word. But occasionally, out of nowhere, we will be clothed with power from on high.

God has not given us power from on high without reason. Rather His disciples are granted power so that they will be His witnesses. The presence and power of God in this fallen world allows us to be unfettered and unhindered. By the power of the Holy Spirit they are going to testify to what Christ accomplished through His life, death and resurrection. Church planting will not take place without this Spirit-given confidence. Without the unsettling work of the Spirit, we all too easily settle for the comfort of the status quo.

Filled with the Holy Spirit, how are we witnesses of what God has done for us in Jesus Christ? Here are four ways in which we are witnesses to Christ in the power of the Spirit.

1. By the Spirit we confess Jesus as Lord

First, 1 Corinthians 12:3 shows us that the Holy Spirit leads us to Jesus as Lord: 'Therefore I want you to understand that no one speaking in the Spirit of God ever says "Jesus is accursed!" and no one can say "Jesus is Lord" except in the Holy Spirit.'

This does not mean that someone who is not a Christian cannot verbalise the words 'Jesus is Lord'. Wicked men can form the words 'Jesus is Lord'. Rather our lives and our mouths testify to the lordship of Jesus Christ through the Holy Spirit. This is the way in which we hold the Father's hand and are occasionally swept up to be kissed.

There is evidence in my life that Jesus is Lord. There are ways that I live and ways that I do not live because Jesus is Lord. There is a way I spend my money and a way I do not spend my money because Jesus is Lord. There is a way I interact with my wife and a way I do not interact with my wife because Jesus is Lord. There is a way I treat God's people and a way I will not treat God's people because Jesus is Lord. We are not men and women who have been unmoved by the abiding presence of the Holy Spirit of God. We have become witnesses in our lives and lips that 'Jesus is Lord'.

If the Spirit does not enthrone Christ in our hearts then we will not give our money for the task for church planting; we will not devote our time; we will not risk our reputations. Churches are planted because the Spirit implants new desires and new priorities in people.

This will always be imperfectly executed. We will always need to throw ourselves on the grace of God. If I am honest there are times when I spend my money the way that Jesus would not spend money. There are times I have addressed my wife in a way that does not reveal that Jesus is my Lord. There have definitely been times that I have addressed the sons and daughters of God in ways that are harsh, unfair, and reveal that there are parts of my heart that still will not testify that Jesus is Lord. But the grace of God gives me the opportunity to repent, confess and have new mercies lavished on me day by day.

2. By the Spirit we live like Jesus

Second, the Holy Spirit empowers us to live like Jesus. Romans 8:11 says: 'If the Spirit of him who raised Jesus from the dead dwells in you, he who raised Christ Jesus from the dead will also give life to your mortal bodies through his Spirit who dwells in you.'

This second point is closely tied to the first. We not only testify that Jesus is Lord, but our lives become more conformed to the image of Jesus Christ. This is at the heart of Romans 8. Romans 8:29 says: 'For those whom he foreknew he also predestined to be conformed to the image of his Son, in order that he might be the firstborn among many brothers.' As sons we are being conformed to the image of Jesus Christ. This is what the Holy Spirit is doing.

One of the misunderstandings about sanctification is that it happens all at once. In fact, it might be more like a crawl. Nevertheless the *you* of today will look more like Jesus than the *you* of two or five or ten years ago. Another mistake is to teach that sanctification looks like strength. In contrast Ed Welch says that 'sanctification looks like weakness'. Sanctification looks like confession, failure and weakness. The Holy Spirit is chiselling us, shaping us, breathing life into us so that we become like Christ. And we are being sanctified not when we look strong and have it all together, but when we cry out to God because we feel in desperate need of His help or when we cry out, 'Not again! Please Lord, forgive me and help me.'

Often people are drawn to the Christlike lives of Christians before they are interested in the message of Christ. Our lives raise the questions to which the gospel is the only answer (1 Pet. 3:15). So the transforming work of the Spirit is not incidental to church planting. Through the Spirit our lives adorn the gospel we preach (Titus 2:10).

3. By the Spirit we are gifted for ministry like Jesus

Third, the Holy Spirit gives us gifts to do ministry like Jesus. John 14:12-16 says:

> Truly, truly, I say to you, whoever believes in me will also do the works that I do; and greater works than these will he do, because I am going to the Father. Whatever you ask in my name, this I will do, that the Father may be glorified in the Son. If you ask me for anything in my name, I will do it.
>
> If you love me, you will keep my commandments. And I will ask the Father, and he will give you another Helper, to be with you for ever.

This passage does not mean that anything Jesus can do, we can do too. My ministry is not played out that way. I often visit hospitals to encourage and pray with people. But I have never walked into a room and told someone they are not sick anymore. Maybe there is a faith issue on my part, although I do lay my hands on people and pray for God to heal, trusting that He is God and His will be done. But I have never walked into the hospital room and shouted, 'Get up! Quit it. You don't have cancer. Get off that bed and follow me.' I have never taken a sandwich, blessed it and fed 5,000 people. When I am in a difficult situation I pray and I expect God to answer. But I do not think that this is what John 14 is teaching. I think the text is teaching us that, as we are formed into churches, we become the presence of the kingdom of God. We perform the works of Christ as we love and serve the poor and sick.

By the Holy Spirit dwelling in us we are witnesses. We are witnesses as we care for the least of these. We accomplish the work of Christ as we multiply our presence among the marginalised. The church enters in where there are those for whom society has no place, no grace, no patience. This is where those who are sealed with the Holy Spirit's power become the very presence of the Son of God.

4. By the Spirit we are reminded of Jesus

Finally, the Bible tells us that the Holy Spirit reminds us of Jesus. In John 14:26 we read: 'But the Helper, the Holy Spirit, whom the Father will send in my name, he will teach you all things and bring to your remembrance all that I have said to you.' Obviously, Jesus was speaking to the apostles, and its primary reference is comforting them in the light of his imminent departure. He assures them of the presence and work of the Spirit in enabling them to teach and write authoritatively as he brings to their minds all that Jesus said and did. The Bible is the means by which we access the words and deeds of Jesus, and the same Holy Spirit that equipped them to write it is the one who illuminates our minds and hearts to read and receive it.

I love this verse because I need to be reminded constantly of what Christ has said and accomplished. I need to be reminded that what God has said is true of me because of Christ. As the old hymn says, 'prone to wander, Lord I feel it.' We can embrace that lyric together because it is a shared experience. But we also praise God because the Holy Spirit reminds us of Jesus. If I am to be a witness then I need to be reminded of what God has said about me in Christ. I often have other thoughts about me – other versions of my identity.

So I need to be reminded what Christ has accomplished. Otherwise I am prone to get caught up with what *I have not* accomplished or take credit for what *He has* accomplished as I try to claim it as my own.

What is God's plan for the purpose and power which the Spirit gives to us? It is that 'you will be my witnesses in Jerusalem'. In Acts 2 we begin to see this happen as Peter preaches the most non-seeker-friendly sermon in the history of Christianity. Peter declares: 'God has made him both Lord and Christ, this Jesus whom you crucified.' (Acts 2:36) And 3,000 people are converted, leading to the creation of the first church of Jerusalem. When Peter speaks again in Acts 3, even more believe. So now there are about 8,000 believers belonging to a distinctly Christian church in Jerusalem. And all the things that are true about church life are true about the church in Jerusalem. When the gospel is preached, some will really love the message and some will hate it. There are those who receive it gladly and there are those who seek to destroy it.

It is also clear that the church has internal issues from the beginning. Ananias and Sapphira see that Barnabas was applauded for selling his land and giving the money to the apostles. So, when they sold land, they claimed to give all the proceeds to the church while in fact keeping some for themselves. That might not look too insidious. But the point is not that the church demanded all their money. Nor is it even that they lied to the church. Peter's accusation is that they lied *to the Holy Spirit*.

There are hundreds of men and women who sit in front of me every week as I preach who have put on the veneer of being

'Christian' but who know nothing of Jesus as Lord and Saviour. These are just good people who are naturally conservative and attach Jesus to their conservative bent. They can speak our jargon. But when caught in adultery or when their marriage is falling apart or when their children are on heroin there is no confession, no cry for help. They go on pretending that everything is OK. That attitude, too, was present in the first church in Jerusalem.

There were also structural issues. In Acts 6:1-7 the Hellenist Jewish widows are being overlooked in the distribution of food. When I preached on this passage in my church I wanted to use it as an opportunity to talk about the crucial issues of racism and cliques. But there is no confession of sin or repentance in the passage. It was an organisational issue that required the church to restructure. They had to be flexible in order to serve the needs of the people. They had to get their structures right. In other words, the Holy Spirit is given not just to enable powerful preaching, but also to sort out the organisational issues that emerge as church plants develop.

At first the church in Jerusalem was just that – the church in Jerusalem. They had no plans to go to Samaria or beyond. But God in His mercy did have a plan. And that plan involved a man being killed. Stephen stands up and, like Peter, once again speaks a very non-seeker-friendly message. He goes through the Old Testament and blames his listeners for everything. The members of the Sanhedrin gnash their teeth, take off their cloaks and lay them at the feet of Saul. Then they pelt Stephen with rocks until he dies. Subsequently a great persecution begins against the believers in Jerusalem. As a result, they scatter, taking the gospel into Samaria. This is not on the agenda of the apostles. But it is the agenda of the Spirit. The Spirit does not simply cause new churches to be planted; the Spirit causes new churches to plant more new churches.

God is sovereign over all things. And so we begin to watch the flame of the gospel spread out from Jerusalem. We see the Spirit enabling churches to be planted across cultural divides. We see Philip speaking to the Ethiopian Eunuch. We see Cornelius being converted. Peter essentially says to him, 'You know I'm not a Gentile sinner like you and so it's illegal for me even to talk to you. But I've had a vision from the Lord and so here I am!' As a result a group of Gentiles are converted and Peter, still reeling from the rebuke of Jesus, understands again that God's plans are bigger than he realised.

The story continues in Acts 13:1-3:

> Now there were in the church at Antioch prophets and teachers, Barnabas, Simeon who was called Niger, Lucius of Cyrene, Manaen a member of the court of Herod the tetrarch, and Saul. While they were worshipping the Lord and fasting, the Holy Spirit said, 'Set apart for me Barnabas and Saul for the work to which I have called them.' Then after fasting and praying they laid their hands on them and sent them off.

From this moment on the focus of the book of Acts moves away from the church at Jerusalem. Instead it follows the missionary journeys of Paul, after he is sent from the church at Antioch. Antioch becomes a model of open-handedness. And once again it is the Holy Spirit who initiates this movement. This is life in the power of the Spirit and it is a missionary life.

One of the things we have said from day one in our church is that no-one is irreplaceable. We have tried to build so that if the Holy Spirit says, 'Send your best teacher and your most courageous miracle worker somewhere else', we can have the heart of Antioch. God is up to something bigger than just the thing He is doing at our church. One of the things I pray for our church is that the really big thing that God is going to do will be in the *next* generation. I hope that what we look at now and think is amazing will actually be just the first fruits of what God will accomplish. Ultimately Antioch becomes the model for all of us, because out of Antioch came missionaries that planted churches that planted churches that made their way to us.

I was converted to Jesus Christ because a guy on my football team said, 'I need to tell you about Jesus. When do you want to do that?' And that happened because for 2,000 years the Holy Spirit has fallen upon men and women who have been willing to go and plant churches. Every time a church plants a church it is opening its hands and saying, 'With the money, people, energy and resources we give you, go to minister where there is no light.'

Churches that plant churches experience loss and gospel goodbyes that are awful and beautiful, right and good. From this we enjoy glory together as we marvel at all that God is doing. Right now there is work at hand. The Holy Spirit is raising up men and we must be open-handed as God calls them to other work, and encourage them as you see giftedness to take on new endeavours.

We are doing this with Beau Hughes. He is a dear friend of mine. I baptised him in the Gulf of Mexico. I have walked with Beau for a long time and he has been on staff at our church for eight years. We meet for lunch regularly. He is one of the most gifted, godly men I have known. He is a faithful elder and servant with a beautiful family. He has brought a seriousness about ecclesiology into the life of our church.

But now we are sending Beau out with a gospel goodbye. I will miss seeing him every day, being in the same trench, and making big decisions with him. But we want to be like Antioch and not like Jerusalem. We want to declare that Jesus' kingdom is better and we do not suffer anything that is not worth it.

The mandate to plant churches is found in the story that led to the point where I got to write this chapter and you got to read it. Through the work of the Spirit the gospel was passed down the generations and spread across the world until it came to us. Then, upon conversion, we received the Holy Spirit's power. We are holding hands with our Father and occasionally we will be clothed in power from on high. We are Christ's witnesses as God conforms us to the image of His Son. We are His witnesses when we testify to His goodness and grace. And we will become His witnesses in Jerusalem, Judea and Samaria, and to the ends of the earth.

It is our turn, whether you have ten, twenty or fifty years of your life left. We are standing on what has been built by the men and women who submitted their lives to Jesus before us. We have the resources and opportunities that have been placed by God into our hands. And as we run forward we must also think of what we will leave for those that follow us.

When we first started our church we did not have any money. Although we were growing, we were growing with twenty-somethings who had a lot of debt and gave change as an offering. So I began to identify gifted young men with a passion for the Lord and paid them almost nothing. One of my hopes for Acts 29 as a global family is that there will be opportunities for young men and women all over the United States to learn what it is like to serve the Lord in different contexts. Even if you have nothing in your hands, you have opportunity, and we have an abundance of opportunity. And we have the Holy Spirit.

7

Multi-ethnic: culture transcending church planting

One Mokgatle

I was going through some old pictures with my wife recently from my early teenage years. With every picture my wife would ask, 'Who's that?' And with every name there was a story which would bring a smile or a chuckle. I was struck by the way each individual had made an impact on my life. After about the tenth picture, my wife said to me, 'You were living a multi-cultural life long before you had a vision to plant a multi-cultural church!'

Each picture was of a person of a different ethnicity, a melting pot of cultures in my photo album. I grew up believing this was the norm, that everyone lived in a context that was diverse and in which everyone embraced this diversity. I couldn't have been further from the truth. That reality hit me when I moved from Botswana to South Africa in 1998, four years after South Africa gained its democratic independence. As I walked through the suburban streets, I felt unwanted, that I didn't belong. It was something I'd never experienced before. Growing up in Botswana I was always surrounded by people of a different colour and socio-economic background. We went to the same schools and shopped at the same grocery stores. Prejudice and racism existed, but they weren't at every corner waiting to pounce, making you feel less than human, stripping you of your dignity. The joy of moving between different circles of different people which I was accustomed to, growing up in the dusty streets of Botswana, learning something new and exciting at every intersection – this joy was slowly fading with every year I lived in South Africa. Despite the fact that the new South Africa was formally becoming more integrated, we were still very much segregated at heart.

Fast forward seventeen years from my first entry into South Africa and things haven't changed much, at least not at a heart level. Certainly much progress has occurred since the late 1990s and of course the change from the apartheid era is like the difference between night and day. Our neighbourhoods, schools and corporate environments are a lot more diverse. But there is still mistrust between the different race groups.

People sometimes say the issue of race relations is the 'elephant in the room'. This idiom captures the sense of there being a glaringly obvious problem that no one wants to discuss. But this idiom hides the seriousness of the issue. When I think about our lack of true, heart-level integration, I don't see a jolly elephant. I see *a roaring lion* seeking to devour whoever is in its path. This lion needs to be caged, not ignored. The matter of race and reconciliation is that serious.

If we continue on the path we're on – simply living past one another – we will continue to build mistrust. And over time this leads to intolerance, bitterness and hate. We need to cross racial, cultural and socio-economic barriers – not just in South Africa, but across the world. We need to learn how to embrace one another's differences so that we might enjoy one another fully in the way we were intended to.

How can we become more diverse, more racially and culturally integrated, especially after so many years of systemic discrimination? I believe the church has to lead in reconciliation. Where policies and regulations fall short, the gospel prospers.

I've always been able to build genuine relationships across different ethnicities and socio-economic groups. This is because of my diverse upbringing and socio-economic privilege. I've always had white friends, black friends, friends who grew up in the suburbs and friends who didn't. But I began to notice that many of them never crossed the line to get to know the other. I wanted them to know the joy I was experiencing as I got to know people from different backgrounds. I felt they were missing out on the beauty of God's rich creation with its different flavours of humanity. So I searched for churches that reflected the diversity of our context. I was disappointed. Though there were churches doing great work, bringing people of all walks of life together, they were few and far between. It was in that gap I felt the Lord calling me to plant a multi-ethnic or transcultural church that would reflect our context and celebrate our diversity.

'Transcultural' is a term I first heard from Léonce Crump Jr and his team at Renovation Church in Atlanta, U.S.A. They've done much to shape my vision and apply it to a South African context. What I mean by a 'transcultural church' is *a community that reflects, embraces and enjoys the diversity of its context, but by the power of the gospel transcends it and creates one new community in Christ.* This is our vision for Rooted Fellowship, our church plant in Pretoria. And our vision is not just to see a transcultural church like this planted, but for it to have a multiplying effect.

I'm often asked why I'm so passionate about this. Why plant a transcultural church in the toughest city in South Africa? The answer is found in the good news of the gospel.

The good news brings people together

Good news brings people together. This is true of any good news. We see fans at local sports pubs celebrating together after the final whistle has blown. People cheer and hug one another – even if they've only just met. Or take another example. How many weddings have you been to where you only know the bridal couple and a handful of other people? Yet at the reception you're on the dance floor with everyone else, partying together like you've known each other for years. Good news brings people together

Bryan Loritts of Trinity Grace Church, New York, says this dynamic is at work in all diverse communities. He goes further: *really* good news brings even strangers together. And, as the bride of Christ, we have the *greatest* news on earth. This news brings people together regardless of ethnicity, culture, age or socio-economic background.

The 'gospel' is good news. That's what the word 'gospel' means. The good news of Jesus Christ is that He came from heaven to live among His creation. He lived the perfect life that we could not live and died a death that you and I deserved to die because of our sin. But the story doesn't end there for He was raised from the dead and ascended to sit at the right hand of the Father. One day He will return to restore all things and fully establish His kingdom. This surely is *good* news – good news that unites strangers!

Paul's ministry displayed this beautifully. Paul would go from city to city preaching the good news of the gospel. In each new context, he would ask two questions. First, he would ask where the synagogue was. He wanted to reach the religious Jews who believed they were God's children by birthright. Second, he would ask where the marketplace and educational institutions were. He wanted to reach those who were considered far from God, the Gentiles. Paul wanted *everyone* to hear the good news, to be transformed by the gospel and to call on Jesus as their Lord and Saviour.

With both Jews and Gentiles coming to faith, it would have been tempting to start two different churches, one for gospel-believing Jews and another for gospel-believing Gentiles. This is what the church has often done throughout history. We tell ourselves this makes sense because we can grow the church bigger more quickly. But Paul didn't start two churches. Paul says: 'Now that you are both in Christ, you are one community.'

The good news destroys the dividing walls in our hearts

In Ephesians 2 Paul explains why the origins of the church are transcultural. In verses 14-16 he talks about the wall that existed between Jew and Gentile. At the time he wrote, this illustration would have resonated powerfully with his readers. For the Jerusalem temple had a literal, dividing wall between Jews and Gentiles. On the walls were inscriptions in Latin and Greek forbidding Gentiles to enter the space of the Jews. Paul says Jesus' death has demolished this wall, allowing Jew and Gentile to worship together.

Of course dividing walls don't just exist in the temple. Dividing walls can also exist in our hearts. But the gospel transforms our hearts. There can be no room for segregation because someone looks different, grew up differently or is in a different socio-economic bracket. Any sense of superiority disappears when we stand together before the cross.

Sadly the church has frequently rebuilt this wall which Christ died to destroy. Martin Luther King Jr once said that the most segregated time in America was 11 o'clock on a Sunday morning. That was fifty years ago. But too often it remains true of our churches in South Africa today. In urban and suburban South Africa our schools are integrated, our places of work are integrated, even our neighbourhoods are integrated. But on Sundays we get in our cars and drive to our homogenous churches to worship the God who has called us to be united in Jesus by the power of His Spirit.

In Paul's day the only place you could see Jew and Gentile coming together in unity was in the church and it blew people's minds. It was a powerful demonstration of the gospel – not just on earth, but also in the heavenly realms. In Ephesians 3:10 Paul says God has united different ethnicities in Christ 'so that through the church the manifold wisdom of God might now be made known to the rulers and authorities in the heavenly places.'

This leaves us with this hard question: In our homogenous circles of comfort are we becoming a hindrance to the gospel? In Revelation 7:9 John sees a vision of 'a great multitude that no one could number, from every nation, from all tribes and peoples and languages, standing before the throne and before the Lamb.' Are we failing to display this beautiful picture of the church as she is meant to be and as she will be? Are people no longer interested in the church because we don't look any different from the local country clubs?

Today people label churches as 'a black church', 'a white church', 'a rich church' or 'a poor church'. This should not be! One of the greatest demonstrations of the gospel is the coming together of people – black, white, rich, poor, male, female, cool, uncool – all coming together because of the good news of the gospel.

Living with differences will be *hard work*. If it were easy, everyone would be doing it. But the gospel transforms our hearts, changing us from enemies of God to children of God. I once heard Derwin Gray, lead pastor of Transformation Church in South Carolina, U.S.A., say: 'Multi-ethnic church is not in *addition* to the gospel; it is a *result* of the gospel.'

Diversity is always possible

The nature of diversity is different in different contexts. If you live in an all-white neighbourhood or an all-black neighbourhood then your local church will reflect that. But there is always diversity in every neighbourhood. There are rich people, poor people, people who vote differently, people who grew up differently. So diversity within the church is always possible.

Many readers will share this conviction that the gospel compels us to move out of our places of comfort to create multicultural churches. You may want to be an advocate for diversity and reconciliation. But you are left with the question, How? How does one apply the gospel to the lives of everyday people who have been shaped by a narrative that promotes segregation?

The answer is the gospel and will always be the gospel. But this gospel must be applied. It's not enough simply to say, 'Preach the gospel and everything else will figure itself out.' Of course we must preach the gospel. But we must also give people the tools to apply it. That doesn't mean some kind of 'seven steps to success' programme. But we must *do* something. The gospel must be lived as well as preached.

Diversity in leaders

One of the most important practical things you can do is strive for a leadership team that reflects the diversity of your context. People often say, 'as goes the pulpit so goes the church.' A community will generally follow the pattern set by its leadership. If what people see at the front is all-white males with skinny jeans, sandals and faded pompadour hairstyles then you'll probably only attract people from that demographic. A diverse leadership team is crucial to begin the journey of building a multi-ethnic church.

Consider the leadership of the church in Antioch: 'Now there were in the church at Antioch prophets and teachers, Barnabas, Simeon who was called Niger, Lucius of Cyrene, Manaen a member of the court of Herod the tetrarch, and Saul.' (Acts 13:1) This leadership team was diverse. It included Barnabas, a Jew and a native of Cyprus. There was Simeon who was black, for 'Niger' is Latin for 'black'. There was another Gentile named Lucius who may have also have been black because he was from Cyrene in North Africa. Also on the team was Manaen who could have been Greek as his name is a Greek form of the Hebrew name 'Menachem'. And then there was Saul, a Jew who had Roman citizenship through his father.

This was no accident. It was the deliberate plan of God, brought to fruition through the power of the gospel. I would have loved to have been a fly on the wall at some of their meetings. I don't think everything was smooth sailing – in and out in thirty minutes with everything on the agenda approved. It would have been challenging because the way individuals engage with the issues reflects their culture and background. But their responses would also have been filtered through the gospel. And often our personal and cultural preferences, when they're filtered by the gospel, return as a 'No'!

We're often tempted to think that homogenous is better. This is a lie. It may be *easier*, but it's definitely not *better*. A diverse leadership forces you to confront these issues and work through them. And that enables you to shepherd your people through the issues.

We have a diverse leadership team in our church and we don't always see eye-to-eye. Most of our differences don't arise from different interpretations of the Bible. They're usually preferences that stem from our different cultural backgrounds. We have to lay these down at the foot of the cross and pray as Jesus prayed, 'Not our will, but the Father's will be done.' It's about *His* kingdom not ours. We're leading *His* people, not ours. So the question we must ask is, 'What will bring the greatest benefit to the church so that they may experience the fulness of God – rather than the 'fullness' of my favourite colour or song?'

Diversity in worship

Diversity in worship style is important in striving for a multi-ethnic church. People have to learn that God is not just praised through traditional hymns or contemporary Christian songs. Other genres can be a sweet fragrance of worship to Him.

We all too easily get stuck with what we like and never stretch ourselves when it comes to music. In our church I had to continually cast the vision of what multi-ethnic worship could look like with a mixture of styles. The vision you need to cast is that in a multi-ethnic church I rejoice with my brothers and sisters even if the music is not my preference. I praise God when I see them worshipping God in a style with which they're familiar. And during the next song they're able to do the same when the style is more to my liking. In this way we begin to live out Ephesians 5:18b-21:

> ... be filled with the Spirit, addressing one another in psalms and hymns and spiritual songs, singing and making melody to the Lord with all your heart, giving thanks always and for everything to God the Father in the name of our Lord Jesus Christ, submitting to one another out of reverence for Christ.

This was a tough battle for us during the early stages of our church plant, not because the music team didn't want to play different genres of music, but because they didn't know how. So we brought in a music consultant to work with our musicians for a few months. They learnt how to use chord substitutions and alternative strumming patterns to produce a different sound. Sometimes a small change can make a big difference to the feel of your music. (Don't be afraid to bring in an unbeliever to help with the musical side of your worship – it could end up being a missional opportunity.)

We were fortunate to have a group of musicians who were willing to be stretched. Like the diverse leadership team, the band must ask, 'Is what we're doing – our song choice and our music style – what will bring the greatest benefit to the church so that they may experience the fulness of God or are we just doing what pleases us as musicians?'

Whatever direction you take, the following principles are key. First, worship is always about God. It's not about the musicians or even the song. It's about the wonder and glory of God. Second, worship is always a congregational act. So everybody must be able to sing together. Songs are often performed at a higher pitch than congregations can sing. But worship is not a performance. If songs are too high, some people will stop singing; the others will stop coming. Let the divas have their moment on their own in the car!

Telling our stories

We need to create in our churches a safe environment where people can share their hearts and learn from each other. In my experience this is the most challenging issue in creating a multi-ethnic church because it touches people's pain and guilt.

In South Africa we generally have two camps. One camp contains people who are filled with anger and bitterness. Either they lived on the receiving end of the brutality and injustice of apartheid or they have horrible stories handed down to them by their parents' generation. The other camp are those who participated in this unjust system or who have benefited from it. They are generally filled with guilt and shame. The challenge is getting both camps talking to each other – not just *at* each other or *over* each other, but genuinely listening to one another.

A mistake we can make as leaders is to gather people to solve problems. Solving problems is important, but you can't solve anything if you don't know what the real issue is. Hearing about racial injustice and prejudice is unbelievably uncomfortable and the temptation is to be defensive rather than to listen. So in our community groups we created a space where people could share their hearts and not feel persecuted.

Every community needs this kind of space, especially when talking about racial reconciliation. I taught people how to show empathy, even when you want to counter what that person is saying with more accurate historical data. Of course, in the pursuit of reconciliation facts have their place. But it's also vital that we listen to one another's pain, hurt, anger, frustration, confusion, guilt, shame and fear. We need to let one another know we are listening. We need to respond by praying for one another, not because that feels like the right thing to do, but because Jesus died on the cross to reconcile us to God and each other.

In our church we simply call this *telling our stories*. Telling our stories has been an important way of acknowledging that we've all been impacted by our country's story. Some have been impacted more than others, but because it's woven into the fabric of our history, it keeps popping up and we can't keep ignoring it. That would be like ignoring the hungry lion in the room. You can only do so for so long before you end up being eaten!

Some amazing things have come out of people telling their stories and being heard.

We've realised that we all have issues, whether we're rich or poor, black or white. We're all broken and in desperate need of a Saviour. This levels the playing field and allows us to start a conversation. Telling our stories has also made us more racially and culturally literate. As we learn about each other, misconceptions and assumptions are dispelled. Of course, there's a lot of stepping on toes and being inappropriate. But if we truly believe we are a family, then we can navigate our way through that awkwardness. I come to realise that the intentions of my brothers and sisters are not to hurt me, but to know me.

Telling stories is never easy, especially in a diverse group. It requires vulnerability and patience. As a leader you will have to display this to your people: be open, and share your own fears, guilt, shame and prejudice. Remind people that God has not given up on them and neither will you. People are at different places on the path and as a leader you have to walk with them. But make sure they are walking. Even baby steps are better than being stationary. Remember: a roaring lion is in the room.

We are striving to be a multi-ethnic church that, by the power of the gospel, will plant more multi-ethnic churches. We want to see this become a movement for the sake of the kingdom to the glory of God. But this is far beyond our abilities or powers to achieve. So prayer must be woven through any attempt to create transcultural communities. The best strategies in the world cannot do what prayer can do. We need supernatural power to see people reconciled to God and then reconciled to each other. So as leaders we must get on our knees and plead with our heavenly Father. Then enjoy the ride! It's often bumpy and sometimes lonely. But Christ has promised never to leave us nor forsake us. And no matter how hard it gets, we know how the story ends:

> After this I looked, and behold, a great multitude that no one could number, *from every nation, from all tribes and peoples and languages*, standing before the throne and before the Lamb, clothed in white robes, with palm branches in their hands, and crying out with a loud voice, 'Salvation belongs to our God who sits on the throne, and to the Lamb!' (Rev. 7:9-10)

8

Men planting churches

STEVE TIMMIS

You would have to have been living on another planet or hiding in a bunker for the last twenty-five years years, not to realise that there are seismic cultural changes underway in the Western world, though other regions are also beginning to feel the tremors. For many of us in many ways the world is barely recognisable from what it was a mere generation ago. The areas where these changes are most apparent are sexuality and gender. Nor should we distinguish these two issues too sharply for they are intimately related.

Increasingly what we might call 'non-differentiation' is the flavour of the day. There is a cultural reaction against the binary opposites which were once viewed as givens. Male and female are no longer seen as helpful biological descriptors. Rather they represent points on a spectrum, along which an individual is free to move as the mood takes her or him. In this undifferentiated world, anything goes. Gender is seen as nothing more than a culturally imposed identity while sexuality has become a matter of mere preference, if not actual choice.

In the 1940s Alfred Kinsey invented the so-called 'Kinsey Scale' which places people on a scale of zero to six according to how they define their sexuality (zero being exclusively heterosexual and six being exclusively homosexual). Surveys based on this scale show that each new generation sees their sexuality as more fluid than the previous generation. According to a 2015 YouGov poll, 43 per cent of 18-24-year-olds define themselves as something other than completely heterosexual or completely homosexual.[1]

This is one reason the issue of complementarianism – the conviction that men and women have complementary roles in the home and church – is so vital. For complementarianism honours the differentiated nature of sexuality and gender. In so doing, it runs contrary to the spirit of the age.

As we look at the different roles for men and women, we take it as read that in Christ men and women are equal in dignity, significance and worth. That does not mean taking them for

---

1. Will Dahlgreen and Anna-Elizabeth Shakespeare, '1 in 2 young people say they are not 100% heterosexual', YouGov.co.uk (16 August 2015), <yougov.co.uk/news/2015/08/16/half-young-not-heterosexual>.

granted. It simply means we are not going to prove what is so clearly true. This equality before God is non-negotiable, incontrovertible and self-evident. Are women ministers of the gospel? For sure! Are they co-labourers and fellow workers? You bet! Can women plant churches? Of course! All of which means that women not only can, but also should be part of a church-planting team. They make a profound, invaluable and significant contribution. Complementarianism celebrates *both* the equality of the sexes *and* the differentiated nature of the sexes – biologically and functionally.

This is how Acts 29 articulates the position (followed by biblical texts on which they are based):

We are deeply committed to the fundamental spiritual and moral equality of male and female and to men as responsible servant-leaders in the home and church.

(1) Both men and women are together created in the divine image and are therefore equal before God as persons, possessing the same moral dignity and value, and have equal access to God through faith in Christ.

(2) Men and women are together the recipients of spiritual gifts designed to empower them for ministry in the local church and beyond. Therefore, women are to be encouraged, equipped, and empowered to utilize their gifting in ministry, in service to the body of Christ, and through teaching in ways that are consistent with the Word of God.

(3) Both husbands and wives are responsible to God for spiritual nurture and vitality in the home, but God has given

to the man primary responsibility to lead his wife and family in accordance with the servant-leadership and sacrificial love characterized by Jesus Christ.

(4) This principle of male headship should not be confused with, nor give any hint of, domineering control. Rather, it is to be the loving, tender and nurturing care of a godly man who is himself under the kind and gentle authority of Jesus Christ.

(5) The Elders/Pastors of each local church have been granted authority under the headship of Jesus Christ to provide oversight and to teach/preach the Word of God in corporate assembly for the building up of the body. The office of Elder/Pastor is restricted to men.

(Gen. 1:26-27; 2:18; Acts 18:24-26; 1 Cor. 11:2-16; Gal. 3:28; Eph. 5:22-33; Col. 3:18-19; 1 Tim. 2:11-15; 3:1-7; Titus 2:3-5; 1 Pet. 3:1-7).

It is important to note what this asserts and what it does not assert.

It is *not* the belief that women are inferior. Quite the opposite. It begins with the conviction that men and women are equally and jointly made in God's image. Men and women are equally guilty of sin and deserving of divine judgment. Men and women are equally the beneficiaries of God's grace in Christ and the object of His atoning death. And men and women are equally the recipients of the Holy Spirit's empowering presence. Churches and church-planting teams need the active involvement of both men and women. Men and women each have indispensable roles to play in the life of the church and its mission in the world. It is demeaning neither sex to assert these roles are distinctive and complementary.

Nor is a complementarian position a defence of patriarchy or male oppression. Two vital assertions should be made at this point.

First, we are talking about headship in the home and in the household of faith. We cannot extrapolate this to a wider society. John Knox may well have dismissed the leadership of Queen Mary by his infamous work, *The First Blast of the Trumpet Against the Monstrous Regiment of Women*. But it is difficult to sustain a coherent biblical argument against women in positions of authority or influence in wider society. In fact, it requires a radical merger or confusion of church and state to do so.

Second, the very opposite of male oppression is being argued here. It is a call to men to take responsibility to serve and nurture their wives in the home and their sisters in the church. The model for headship is the Lord Jesus Christ and specifically His sacrificial love demonstrated at the cross (Eph. 5:25-27). Jesus our Bridegroom took responsibility for His bride, offering His very life that she might flourish. He put her relationship with God before His own. He died forsaken by God that His church might be united to God.

A complementarian position is a recognition that God has made men and women different. There is not one gender. Nor is gender a continuum with multiple or malleable graduations of femininity and masculinity. Of course, we need to beware of false cultural assumptions about what femininity and masculinity involve. But the Bible is clear that God has created two distinctive genders – 'male and female he created them' (Gen. 1:27).

With these distinctive genders come distinctive roles in both home and church. Again, we must not exaggerate this. Men and women in the body of Christ have more in common than we have in distinction. We are called to the same faith, to the same love, to the same hope. Nevertheless we are given different roles. I am persuaded biblically that headship is male. In the home the husband is called to lead. This means taking responsibility for creating and nurturing an environment in which those under his care flourish. In the church pastors are likewise tasked with creating an environment for others to flourish to the glory of God. In the church women are called to serve the Lord gladly (along with the majority of men who are not elders) in glad and humble submission to (male) elders. There is nothing coerced about this submission. It is to be done willingly as part of her discipleship and out of reverence for Christ. It is striking that in the household codes in Ephesians and Colossians, Paul addresses the women directly and calls them to submit 'as to the Lord' (Eph. 5:22) and 'as is fitting in the Lord' (Col. 3:18).

This means that men should take the primary responsibility for the teaching and preaching of God's word. This is stated explicitly in 1 Timothy 2:12: 'I do not permit a woman to teach or to exercise authority over a man; rather, she is to remain quiet.' But it is also the logical extension of male leadership. This is an important part of the argument. In the church leadership is exercised through the preaching and teaching of God's word. Elders do not have authority simply because of their office.

They exercise Christ's authority by proclaiming Christ's word. Their authority is derivative. It is derived from Christ through His word. This is the limit and extent of their authority. Their authority is limited to the exercise of God's word – they cannot simply tell people what to do according to their own whim. But what authority this is, for it is the authority of Christ Himself.

What does this mean in practice? The complementarian conviction of Acts 29 provokes a number of questions of application because it necessarily leaves open a range of issues:

- Can a woman be a member of staff in a church?

- Can a woman have an executive role that involves overseeing the work of men?

- Can a woman be given the title 'Pastor' over a designated area of ministry? Or should she be referred to as 'Director' or 'Co-ordinator'?

- In what contexts, if any, can a woman teach or preach?

- Can a woman lead or co-lead a small group?

- Can a woman lead the corporate worship of the gathered church?

- Can a woman baptise or administrate communion?

- Can a woman serve as a deacon?

- Can a woman speak at a conference attended by men and women?

Without in any way minimising these questions, we should note that there are two extremes to which complementarians sometimes resort to answer them. Some feel uneasy about placing any significant restrictions on women. So they allow women to do pretty much whatever men can do. This is what we might call 'formal complementarianism' (in contrast to a functional complementarianism). Other people eliminate the problem by allowing women no significant role at all. This is what we might call 'fearful complementarianism' (in contrast to a thankful complementarianism). Neither of these positions is faithful to the text of the Bible.

How one resolves some of the questions raised above depends to some extent on one's attitude towards the so-called regulative principle. The regulative principle states that in the life of the church we should only do what the Bible commands or what can be derived from the explicit teaching of Scripture. In other words, activities require an explicit precedent in the Bible to be a legitimate part of church life. In contrast to this is what is sometimes known as the normative principle. This states that we can do anything the Bible does *not* forbid. Activities require no explicit permission in the Bible to be a legitimate part of church life. For example, can a woman baptise someone? Adherents of the regulative principle might answer 'No' since this is not explicitly mandated in the Bible. Adherents of the normative principles might answer 'Yes' since it is not explicitly forbidden in the Bible.

These different approaches, along with differences in how they should be applied, create grey and fuzzy areas. In these areas we can and should allow one another gospel freedom. Different churches will make different judgments on these matters in good conscience.

But these ambiguities do not mean everything is ambiguous. The Bible is clear that the role of pastor or elder is restricted to men, and when authority is exercised through the teaching or preaching of the Bible that should be done by men.

Does this matter? Why is this a foundational conviction of Acts 29? Why can it not be left to the conviction of individual churches? After all, those who maintain a paedo-baptist position within Acts 29 hold their convictions on baptism for biblical reasons. Yet they are happy to partner with those who hold a credobaptist position. And vice versa. So why make complementarianism a distinctive of Acts 29? Why is complementarianism important for the health of local churches and church-planting teams? Why not regard it as a secondary issue about which we can allow freedom for the sake of gospel unity?

After all a complementarian view is not central to the gospel. It does not sit alongside the incarnation of Christ, His full humanity and divinity, His death on the cross bearing the penalty of His people's sin as our substitute, the physical resurrection and ascension of Jesus to receive all authority from the Father, justification by faith alone, the sending of the Spirit to empower the church for mission, the return of Christ, the final judgment and the promise of eternal life. Complementarianism is not one of these cardinal truths.

Bruce Ware helpfully suggests complementarianism is central today for two reasons.[2]

---

2. Bruce Ware, 'Gender Moves?' in *Evangelicals Now* (June 2015), <e-n. org.uk/2015/06/features/gender-moves>.

1. A cultural fault line

First, Ware says: 'This doctrine is central strategically in upholding the Christian faith within a culture all too ready to adopt values and beliefs hostile to orthodox and evangelical conviction.'

The battle lines today between the Christian faith and the surrounding culture, he suggests, are not primarily doctrinal. The world is not debating the virgin birth of Christ or his physical resurrection, the authority of Scripture or the means of justification. Instead the pressure points today are gender and sexuality. The relativism of our postmodern culture cares little for doctrinal affirmations. It is happy for us to believe whatever we want. But it will not tolerate dissent from its sexual and egalitarian agenda.

The issue of gender roles is ethical rather than doctrinal. Egalitarianism is not a heresy. Yet to compromise at this point is to allow the culture to set the agenda for the church. Our thinking becomes driven by the culture rather than the word of God. And that sets us on a trajectory that will lead to doctrinal compromise.

The pressure is clearly growing on the church to compromise in these areas. And this pressure increases as parts of the church capitulate. So the temptation to argue that we can show flexibility because this issue is not a primary doctrine increases.

But the world is not looking for a ready accommodation with the church. That is not its intent. Unbelievers are not hoping for a few tweaks to Christian practice that will pave the way for them to re-join the church in large numbers. Our post-Christian culture will keep on pushing an agenda that validates its rebellion against God.

The call of the New Testament is not to be like the world. Its call is to be holy, to be distinctive. Romans 12:2 says: 'Do not be conformed to this world, but be transformed by the renewal of your mind, that by testing you may discern what is the will of God, what is good and acceptable and perfect.' Our goal is not conformity to the world, but transformation through God's word. Our goal is not the will of the world, but the will of God.

2. A gospel pattern

Second, Ware argues that complementarianism is central because marriage is a picture of the gospel itself. Marriage, according to Paul in Ephesians 5:31-32, was designed by God to reflect the relationship between Christ and His people. The life-long covenant commitments of marriage point to God's enduring covenant commitment to the church. So marriage and gender roles are not social or cultural constructs. They are divinely revealed. And they are also *revealing* in the sense that they are given by God as a revelation of his passionate commitment to His people. They point to the gospel. And, if they are designed by God, we are not free to redesign them.

Of course Christian egalitarians uphold the sanctity of marriage. But in Ephesians 5 Paul does not simply say *that* marriage points to the relationship of Christ to His people. He also says *how* it points to that relationship. The wife submits to her husband so that she pictures the church's submission to Christ. And the husband is to love his wife so that he pictures

Christ's love for His bride. It is not marriage in general that illustrates Christ's union with the church. It is marriage with male headship, sacrificial, reciprocating love and female submission. To redefine the gender relationships within marriage is fatally to blur the picture that marriage presents.

A missional stance

Complementarianism matters because complementarianism is missional. Behind all the contributions to this book is the conviction that the church is God's primary mission strategy in the world. In line with this, our task is to litter the world with communities of light, for that is how the darkness is penetrated and dispelled by the gospel. For this to happen, the church needs to be formed by the gospel and to exist for the gospel. That impacts not merely the message we proclaim, but also the medium through which it is proclaimed. As the 'body of Christ', the church gives shape, texture and hue to the gospel.

The local church, to the extent to which she lives her life before the world, puts the gospel on display in a given context and helps those outside better understand the truths it celebrates. For example, justification becomes explicable as the people of God rest in Christ and do not attempt to justify themselves through careers, achievements or hobbies. Forgiveness becomes attractive as the people of God bear with each other's weaknesses, turn the other cheek and forgive 'seventy times seven'. The indiscriminate invitation of the gospel becomes compelling as the people of God takes an open-arm stance to the world and welcomes even the worst of sinners into her midst.

Complementarianism comes into this category. It displays something vital, true and pertinent about God. It gives a glimpse into the inner-life of the Trinity. It displays a beautiful equality along with an intimate, complementary dependency. As husbands lead in the home and as elders lead in the church, they express something of the nature of the Father's leadership. As elders shepherd the flock, they provide an insight into the Shepherd's heart. As wives submit to their husbands' leadership, they show the world a bold and beautiful humility.

When we consider how the plan of redemption was conceived and accomplished, and it is so effectively applied, we should stand in awe at the Father, Son and Holy Spirit. We should marvel at their wisdom and be overwhelmed by the efficiency with which they each contribute their part. But most of all, we should be thankful for their stunning co-operation and willingness to prefer and defer.

This is what complementarianism does. This is what should be expressed in the churches we plant all around the world. This is theology with clothes on. This is truth with style. Only the gospel creates it. And the whole world is waiting for it.

9

Women planting churches

RUTH WOODROW

Where does a complimentarian conviction leave women when it comes to planting churches? Do women have a role in church planting?

I am part of a church plant. And I am part of a gospel community within that church plant which is seeking to reach Muslims. So I spend a good proportion of my time with Muslim women.

The Quran's voice is the voice of a man. The Quran is written to men. Women in Islam are subject to men and are only relevant in terms of their relationships to men. Only being a wife or a mother makes something of you. Only this gives you purpose. Otherwise you are irrelevant within Islam. Muslims believe that if you marry a woman when she is very young – and that essentially when she is a child – it is beneficial for you. The Muslim view of paradise is that every man will receive a group of virgins given for their pleasure. This is an eschatology for men. But what if you are a woman? What on earth is your service to God for? Women in Islam are taught to serve God. But it is not *for* anything.

In the West we live in an increasingly feminised culture. But in reality this is not an improvement for women. Women are expected to perform in the workplace, in the home and in bed. We are pulled between our careers and our children. Anxiety about body image is widespread. Our looks and our appearance are constantly scrutinised and commented on. We live in a world that does not know what to do with women. We think we have sorted it out in the West and think the East is horrific in its attitude to women. But women in the West are not finding a place of purpose and fulfilment.

It is only through the gospel that women find a place of true value and purpose. Women do have a place within ministry. The church should be the place where women can flourish, where they are valued, where they are cared for and where they can find fulfilment.

The vision for women in creation

Genesis 1:26-27 says:

> Then God said, 'Let us make man in our image, after our likeness. And let them have dominion over the fish of the sea and over the birds of the heavens and over the livestock and over all the earth and over every creeping thing that creeps on the earth.'
>
> > So God created man in his own image,
> > in the image of God he created him;
> > male and female he created them.

Right at the start women are mentioned, women are addressed, and women are acknowledged as being created in God's image. Women are image-bearers.

In Genesis 2 Adam is given the job of cultivating the garden. And we discover he needs a helper. We see here that women have a place at the heart of the cultural mandate. We are included in the work that has to be done. Adam and Eve together are to live by the word of God in community with each other and with God in the context of every day. Adam and Eve were to partner together as they worked, as they rested, as they looked after and enjoyed the creation. And this job was worldwide in its scope. The task given to women does not stop at the front door.

So women are involved in culture-creation and culture-cultivation at every level alongside men. That includes creativity, arts, crafts, fine art, medicine, engineering and so on. Wherever culture is developing, there is a place for women with men to be developing the world in the image of their Creator.

Plenty of the people outside the church and some inside the church believe Christianity says the woman's sphere of influence is limited to the home. Homemaking is a very valuable thing that women are often very good at. I am a homemaker myself. But the idea that all women can do is homemaking and catering does not fit this vision of creation. This is clearly not where our role is supposed to start and stop. A woman is supposed to image her Creator wherever she is and whatever the work is which God has given her to do.

We see this beautifully illustrated in the description of 'the excellent wife' in Proverbs 31. This woman embodies what it means to be an image-bearer. She enjoys creation. She works with her hands. She engages in business. She cares for her family. She is right there alongside her husband at every level of cultural engagement.

In Genesis 2:18 the LORD says: 'It is not good that the man should be alone.' It is as men and women together that we bear God's image. This passage refers specifically to marriage. But the implication is that the world is not supposed to be full of men. God designed the world to have women in it. That means there is an essential purpose to be fulfilled by women. The world would be worse if there were no women! And it is God who makes that declaration.

In Genesis 3 Eve listens to the Serpent's lies about God, and Adam joins her. They listen to a word that is not God's word. They no longer live under God's word. As a result, the community between them is broken and the community between them and God is broken. Everyday life descends into carnage.

Ever since, women have faced trouble. Because they are no longer living under God's word, they become unhappy with the purpose God has for them. They want to go it alone. Eve believed she was obtaining freedom for herself in this moment. In fact she and her daughters have experienced nothing but slavery ever since. She thought she was buying herself freedom, but she was enslaving herself to her own view of the world and walking away from life under God's wise counsel.

Today women face forced slavery in many parts of the world. In the West we are in a kind of voluntary slavery. It is voluntary, but it is slavery none the less. Nobody is free. Only the gospel can liberate us from this situation. The gospel brings us back to be the women we were supposed to be with a divinely gifted sense of purpose and fulfilment.

A restored vision for women in redemption

This vision of a humanity restored through the gospel is what we see in Colossians 3:1-17:

> If then you have been raised with Christ, seek the things that are above, where Christ is, seated at the right hand of God. Set your minds on things that are above, not on things that are on earth. For you have died, and your life is hidden with Christ in God. When Christ who is your life appears, then you also will appear with him in glory.
>
> Put to death therefore what is earthly in you: sexual immorality, impurity, passion, evil desire, and covetousness, which is idolatry. On account of these the wrath of God is coming. In these you too once walked, when you were living

in them. But now you must put them all away: anger, wrath, malice, slander, and obscene talk from your mouth. Do not lie to one another, seeing that you have put off the old self with its practices and have put on the new self, which is being renewed in knowledge after the image of its creator. Here there is not Greek and Jew, circumcised and uncircumcised, barbarian, Scythian, slave, free; but Christ is all, and in all.

Put on then, as God's chosen ones, holy and beloved, compassionate hearts, kindness, humility, meekness, and patience, bearing with one another and, if one has a complaint against another, forgiving each other; as the Lord has forgiven you, so you also must forgive. And above all these put on love, which binds everything together in perfect harmony. And let the peace of Christ rule in your hearts, to which indeed you were called in one body. And be thankful. Let the word of Christ dwell in you richly, teaching and admonishing one another in all wisdom, singing psalms and hymns and spiritual songs, with thankfulness in your hearts to God. And whatever you do, in word or deed, do everything in the name of the Lord Jesus, giving thanks to God the Father through him.

This passage provides an answer to our question about the role of women. If you are a Christian then you have died with Christ, you have been raised with Christ and you are now part of the new community described in this passage. In verse 12 we see it is a community whose members let the word of God dwell richly among them. It is a community whose members bear with one another, forgive each other, love each other. Through the death, resurrection and ascension of Jesus we become a people of the word again. We are a people living by the word of Christ in community in the context of everyday life.

According to verse 10 we are to 'put on the new self, which is being renewed in knowledge after the image of its creator'. Through the gospel we are being restored to become the women of Genesis 1 and 2 again. In other words, through the gospel women are in a position where they are working as partners alongside men. And for this we need:

- to be living by the word of Christ …

- in community with each other and in community with God …

- in the context of the every day.

In the second half of Colossians 3 Paul talks specifically about the roles of women and the roles of men. In Colossians 3 and Ephesians 5 women are to submit within the marriage relationship, and in 1 Timothy 2–3 we see the overseeing and teaching of churches is a role for men.

But the Bible is not like the Quran. The Bible *does* address women. Everything else that is written in the New Testament is written to believers including women. Everything else that is commanded is commanded of women as well as men. Everything in Colossians 3:1-17 is for women.

When we read in Colossians 3, for example, about 'teaching and admonishing one another in all wisdom' it is talking to women as well as men. We hear the words of Jesus: 'Go therefore and make disciples of all nations' (Matt. 28:19). They are addressed to women as well as men.

If you are a believer then these passages are addressed to you. This means there is no 'get out'. Women are to be making disciples. Women are to be all about the fame of Jesus. This is what we are for. This has always been what we were supposed to be for. So there should be a fire in your belly for proclaiming, teaching and defending the gospel. This is to be your role wherever you can and whenever you can – every minute of every hour of every day of every year of your life. Every moment must be lived in passionate service to our Saviour and King.

Jesus has risen from the dead and given you a sure hope of resurrection. He is at the right hand of the Father declaring you righteous, saying, 'You and you and you are a princess in my kingdom. Be princesses in my kingdom.' So contend for joy in Jesus – for yourself and for others. This is what you are supposed to do. This is your role.

Paul applies this general principle to specific roles in the second half of Colossians 3. So if you are married then your marriage is about King Jesus. It is not about you. It has never been about you. Your marriage is not about your husband making much of you. Nor is it about you making much of your husband. It is about Jesus. You need to be passionate about making much of Jesus and you need to be passionate about your husband doing the same. This is what marriage is for. Your marriage is a partnership for the service of God, just as it was in Genesis 2.

If you have children you need to teach them that nothing is more important to you than Jesus and nothing should be more important to them than Jesus. You need to show that the only path to joy is with Jesus. Fight for joy in Jesus in your home.

If you are not married then fight for joy in Jesus. Do not waste a single moment of the life that Jesus bought through

His precious blood by being preoccupied with the desire for marriage. It will be a waste. Instead fight for joy in Jesus – your joy in Jesus and other people's joy in Jesus. Colossians 3:15-17 says:

> And let the peace of Christ rule in your hearts, to which indeed you were called in one body. And be thankful. Let the word of Christ dwell in you richly, teaching and admonishing one another in all wisdom, singing psalms and hymns and spiritual songs, with thankfulness in your hearts to God. And whatever you do, in word or deed, do everything in the name of the Lord Jesus, giving thanks to God the Father through him.

In our churches and in our families we need to keep our eyes open. When you look at your marriage, your family, your church, do you see peaceful, thankful people? Do you see people who dwell on the word of God as they teach and admonish each other? Do you see people loving Jesus and enjoying joy because of Jesus? Where you do, praise God and offer words of encouragement. Where you do not, there is work for you to do.

Are you equipped with the words so you can teach and admonish with wisdom? Are you yourself resting in the word so you can detect when things have lost their gospel trajectory? Can you look at someone's life or marriage or parenting and know that it is not going in the direction of Jesus? Wherever there is a place to teach and admonish with wisdom, there is a place for you as a woman to minister the gospel.

Men, wherever there is a place to teach and admonish with wisdom, there is a place for women in your churches to minister the gospel and a place for you to encourage and equip them to do that.

Hebrews 3:12-13 says you are to take care 'lest there be in any of you an evil, unbelieving heart, leading you to fall away from the living God'. There is a danger that Christians might 'be hardened by the deceitfulness of sin'. The solution is to 'exhort one another every day'.

Are you watching for those who are faltering? Are you ready to exhort others with truth so that hearts are not deceived by sin? This passage is significant because it assumes a rich picture of community in which people are seeing each other every day. Again, you need to ask yourself, Are you familiar with the people in your church and the issues they are facing? Are you asking questions that explore people's hearts?

There are no boundaries here for women. We are all called to campaign for joy in Christ and wisdom in the gospel in everyone around us – and that includes men, women and children alike.

Women need to encourage the men around them to be good stewards of the gospel. You want to see them flourish into men who can step into their gospel responsibilities. You want to grow them into leaders.

I have two sons. And I want them to grow up to be men of the gospel. I want them to grow past me into leadership over me. That is what I am campaigning for. My daughters will always be younger women to me. But I hope my sons will grow to one day lead over me. So teach boys to take gospel responsibility. Raise up a generation of leaders for the church.

When the Serpent comes to Eve in the Garden of Eden, Adam just stands by. The snake is telling lies about God. Adam should have said, 'Stop telling lies about God.' He should have stamped on the snake. But that is not what Eve should have done. It was not her role to stamp on the Serpent and defy his lies. Eve should have said, 'Adam?' Adam starts his job well enough because, while Eve was not there when God gave the first command in the garden, Eve knew what the command was. So Adam had already taught his wife. So, when the Serpent comes, Eve should have said: 'Adam, you told me God says we are not to eat from the tree. You said this was the way to live with blessing. You said our job was to rule and protect the garden. But there are lies in the garden now. Someone is lying to me about God.' Eve, if necessary, should have done that for the rest of her life. Adam was given the job of protecting the Garden from the snake. But she was supposed to help him with every breath she had.

It is the same for us. We all know that women are brilliant at nagging. But we have a carte blanche to do *gospel*-nagging. So let us redeem nagging! Let us be people who have nothing to say and nothing to do except contend for Jesus. I want to see men become good leaders. I want to see men take responsibility. I want to see people flourish. I want to contend for the fame of Jesus in the way God has given me to do it.

Women in the community of the church

What does this look like in practice? Here are two examples from our context.

1. Home-schooling together

I am a home-schooling mum with four children. I home-school with two other families in our church community. I assure you it can be crazy! Our houses are not large so space is limited and at times we have eleven children between us. We teach our children together. But the primary purpose is to get our children together so we can work together as mothers. We talk about our relationships, the relationships we have with unbelievers, what is going on with our children. It is also an opportunity to see each other parent our children and to be involved in the lives of one another's children. In our times together I suspect an outsider might not be able to tell which children belong to which parent. That is because we teach each other's children and take responsibility for each other's children. Just last week there were some situations with a couple of the children. So we abandoned the educational curriculum. The mother was despairing. She did not know what to do with them. So we talked about what would be the best next steps.

2. Learning together

I like to eat. And I have had an on-going conversation with a young elder in our congregation who is a personal trainer. We talk a lot about what it means to be wise with food. We talk about what it means to enjoy food while not getting drawn into the 'do not taste, do not touch' approach that the word of God warns us against in Colossians 2:20-23. We talk about what it means to be wise and not to be ruled by our stomachs. That conversation has gone backwards and forwards for some time. As a result we have both grown in wisdom. I do not think there is anything inappropriate in us having that conversation together. We are teaching each other. Meanwhile he is drawing on those conversations and turning them into useful teaching for others. I am not trying to replace him or usurp his authority. We are learning together and as a result he is being equipped to lead. As a result we all have benefited within our church community.

Women in the mission of the church

The world around you is full of people who do not know Jesus. They do not know His peace and rest. They do not know the joy and sanity which the gospel brings. It is light years from their experience.

This is why we want to plant churches and this is why as women we should want to be part of planting churches. You do not need to have a function or a job title or a salary. You do not need to be called a leader or a pastor to get on with the task of mission. Meet people and share the gospel with them.

So my questions are these. Are you sharing your home with unbelievers? Are you sharing your meals with them? Are you listening for, and answering, their questions? Are you encouraging others to do the same?

What does this look like in practice? Here are two more simple examples from our context.

My gospel community is particularly focused on trying to reach British Asians. I live in an area in which about 50 per cent of the people are from an Asian background, mostly families from Bangladesh. We deliberately live among our Muslim neighbours. We are friends with them. We have built relationships with them.

Every Wednesday afternoon all the women in my gospel community (with the exception of one woman who is single and has a full-time job) meet in my house. It is packed! We feed our children together. Then we pray together for the people we are getting to know, who do not know the Lord. We farm our children out to as many rooms as we can for a rest (that is an essential). And then we do some craft activities together and invite our Muslim women friends to join us. Some women would like to come, but are not allowed. Others come from time to time. When no-one comes, we often pray instead for the women we know. We pray that we would find other opportunities with these women. The key thing is we have made a commitment together as a gospel community to have that time dedicated to getting alongside those Muslim women.

The wife of another one of our elders does not home-school her children. Her children are in a local school and so she plans her school run in a missional way. She is brilliant at it. She ensures there is the greatest 'surface area' around her that there can possibly be to offer the maximum possible exposure to the gospel to other parents. She never takes her children to school by herself. She always knocks on the door of the people in the community around her who take their children to the same school so they can walk together. Or she helps other families by taking their children to school and back for them. She is intentional about whom she is talking to and making relationships so she can create opportunities to talk about Jesus.

Making disciples includes both those around you who are believers *and* those around you who are not yet believers.

Contend for joy in the gospel in the lives of those who are not yet believers. Fight for it. We have coined a phrase in our church: We should be 'fierce women', fierce for the gospel. Or sometimes we speak of 'gentle warriors'.

10

Conclusion

STEVE TIMMIS

For all the talk about church planting, I'm not entirely convinced that it has really taken root in the collective consciousness of contemporary evangelicalism. You only have to look at the number of churches that *don't* plant to see that. But add to that the number of churches that have planted only infrequently, despite their size and resources. Indeed some may have planted reluctantly; certainly hesitantly. And how many experienced church leaders leave an established church to plant other churches? I know of almost none. If it happened often then I guarantee that the level of church planting would rise exponentially.

Every church that exists has at some time been planted. Of course, it has happened for a whole range of reasons: some good, some bad and some just downright ugly. But one way or another every church has been planted. Shouldn't that fact alone dispose us to the task? Apparently not.

What about the hard facts? In a survey of 350 churches conducted by Challenge 2000 just prior to the new millennium, it was found that the sixty-four churches planted in the previous decade had grown by an average of 75 per cent per year. By contrast, even the strong evangelical and charismatic churches established prior to that date were increasing at just 6 per cent each year. New church plants were growing twelve times as fast as established churches. In addition, 68 per cent of the growth in the new congregations was from conversions and renewals with only 25 per cent from transfers.

Facts like these support the assertion that church planting is the most effective evangelistic strategy. Yet the last fifteen years have not seen evangelicals press on with any degree of urgency or creativity. The prevailing model of church planting is still of a church of a reasonable size, sending a sizeable group with a pastor. Please don't misunderstand me. This is great when it happens. I have absolutely no criticism to make of that model. My problem is that it's the dominant model. We should be thrilled when it happens. But other models should excite the imagination.

So in this conclusion I want to return to the book of Acts to glean what kind of church planting actually took place in the early days of the church and lessons we can learn for church planting today.

Let me start by headlining a principle that comes out in the book of Acts: churches are the *result* of mission and the *means* of mission. This is why churches need to be planted.

As we saw in chapter 3, the narrative of the book of Acts is divided into six sections, each with its own geographical focus and each concluding in a summary statement highlighting the growth of the gospel.

1:1–6:7	Jerusalem (with a summary statement in 6:7)
6:8–9:31	Judea, Samaria & Galilee (with a summary statement in 9:31)
9:32–12:24	the coastlands to Syria (with a summary statement in 12:24)
12:25–16:5	Cyprus and Galatia (with a summary statement in 16:5)
16:6–19:20	Macedonia, Achaia and Asia (with a summary statement in 19:20)
19:21–28:31	Rome (with a summary statement in 28:31)

Let's take a swift tour, following this journey with Luke as he takes us from Jerusalem to Rome. What we will discover is that church planting is far from an incidental feature in the unfolding drama. Wherever the gospel bears fruit, a church is planted.

On the Day of Pentecost 3,000 people were converted (Acts 2:37-41). Then immediately Luke describes their communal life (2:42-47). The disciples bear witness to Christ through both their words and their lives as Jesus commands them in the programmatic statements of 1:8. And as a result a church (or multiple churches, depending on your definitions) is planted. The description of this post-Pentecost corporate life shows the initial impact of that witness-bearing in Jerusalem. And we find all of the elements contained in the Great Commission. New believers were baptised on profession of faith (2:41) and apostolic teaching so they might be discipled (2:42). They met together and shared life on a daily basis (2:46). Following Jesus was a lifestyle rather than merely a decision, and the result was further gospel expansion (2:47).

After Stephen's death, persecution resulted in the church in Jerusalem being 'scattered throughout the regions of Judea and Samaria' (8:1). Luke tells us that 'those who had been scattered went about preaching the word' (8:4), including Philip. Philip preached the gospel in Samaria and as a result a church was planted among the Samaritans. We know this because in 9:31 Luke records that, after Saul's conversion, 'the church throughout all Judea and Galilee and Samaria enjoyed peace, being built up; and going on in the fear of the Lord and in the comfort of the Holy Spirit, it continued to increase' (NASB). The church preached the gospel as it was scattered and as a result a church was planted. The 'church' increased as local congregations were established in the regions of Judea, Galilee and Samaria. All these congregations were planted from Jerusalem, but not necessarily by Jerusalem – although they almost certainly retained some sort of relationship with Jerusalem and its leadership.

In Acts 10 a hugely significant event occurs when Peter is sent to Cornelius, the Roman centurion. Cornelius and his household are Gentiles. God prepares Peter for this move with a recurring vision in which a voice declares: 'What God has made clean, do not call common' (Acts 10:15). This incident paves the way for the proclamation of the gospel and the planting of churches in the Gentile world.

In Acts 11:19-26 we learn how the gospel came to Antioch, a city about 300 miles north of Jerusalem. It happened without any planning or strategy. It was simply the result of believers speaking about Jesus to anyone and everyone. Spontaneously, a large group of people, mainly Gentiles apparently, turn to the Lord. These were clearly not a disconnected assortment of individuals, because a collective identity had formed by the time Barnabas arrives from Jerusalem. We are not told why Barnabas was dispatched, but he was encouraged by what he saw, and started to encourage them. He also gets Saul involved in what is happening and Luke matter-of-factly records that 'they met with the church and taught considerable numbers' (11:26 NASB). Again we see that where the gospel bears fruit, a church is planted.

In Acts 13 we see how Antioch became a church-planting church as they responded to the Holy Spirit, and they commission Paul and Barnabas to take the gospel into the world. Due to the faithfulness of those church leaders, churches are planted in Derbe, Lystra and Iconium. On the outward journey Paul and Barnabas preach the gospel and see people converted. Then on the return journey they appoint leaders in what Luke is now calling churches (14:23).

As the story continues so the momentum gathers. The first church in Europe was established in Philippi (16:11-40).

Churches were then planted in Thessalonica and Berea (17:1-15), Corinth and Ephesus (18:1-11; 19:1-10). We are told of churches in Troas (20:7-12), Tyre (21:3-5), Ptolemais (21:7) and Caesarea (21:8-14). When later Paul reached Rome (28:15-16), there was already a church in place. From the remainder of the New Testament, we know of churches in Colossae, Laodicea (Col. 4:16), Thessalonica, throughout Crete (Titus 1:5), Pontus, Cappadocia, Asia and Bithynia (1 Pet. 1:1), Smyrna, Pergamum, Thyatira, Sardis and Philadelphia (Rev. 1:11). By the end of the New Testament period new churches not only litter the narrative, but much of the land mass to the north of the Mediterranean.

Wherever the gospel went, new churches started. This is the New Testament model of gospel expansion. If the Great Commission sets our agenda, evangelism is about either incorporating new believers into churches or starting new churches with them. Paul's methodology focused on church planting. Church planting was not a by-product of his evangelism, but central to it. In Acts church planting is not a traumatic event with a long lead in time. There is nothing odd or out of the ordinary about it. It does not happen circumstantially, but constantly and normally. In the same way, church planting should be as much a part of the thinking of our churches as everything and anything else we do. According to Jesus, our goal is not to win converts but to make disciples – and making disciples means planting churches!

Having established the centrality of church planting to apostolic mission, we are now in a position to look at how these churches were actually started. I want to draw out six principles. They don't add up to a 'How To', but they will help us practically in the always varied, often difficult and sometimes convoluted process of planting churches.

1. Preach the gospel

One thing we know for certain is that Paul went around the Mediterranean preaching the gospel. This was how believers were gathered (Acts 13:5; 13:7; 13:44; 17:13). Paul's statement in Acts 20:24 serves as a summary of his ministry: 'I consider my life worth nothing to me, if only I may finish the race and complete the task the Lord Jesus has given me—the task of testifying to the gospel of God's grace' (NIV). All the churches planted after Antioch were done so because Paul preached the gospel in every place and at every opportunity. Paul's words to the church in Corinth, in the opening chapter of his first letter, makes that plain enough. Why did the Risen Jesus commission Paul? 'To preach the gospel' of 'Jesus Christ and him crucified' (1 Cor. 1:17; 2:2).

This might seem a 'no-brainer', but there is nothing more important in church planting than keeping the gospel clear and keeping it central. Luke tells us Paul stayed in Corinth for eighteen months, teaching the word of God (Acts 18:11). The context shows he is not merely describing his evangelism. The gospel that saves is the gospel that sanctifies, so a lot is at stake if your 'gospel' isn't actually the gospel. Tim Keller puts it this way:

> We must never forget that Jesus was full of grace and truth (John 1:14). Truth without grace is not really truth, and grace

without truth is not really grace. Any religion or philosophy of life that de-emphasizes or loses one or the other of these truths falls into legalism or into licence. Either way, the joy and power and release of the gospel are stolen – by one thief or the other.[1]

The gospel is the good news of God's grace. It is the message that focuses on what God has done in Christ. The gospel says that in the life, death and resurrection of Jesus God has done it all. There is nothing, absolutely nothing, anyone can do to contribute to their salvation. Understanding the gospel keeps us from both arrogant superiority and spineless cowardice. The gospel is what people, including 'our' people, need to hear. And only the gospel can produce the community of sinner-saints known as the church of God.

2. Understand the context

Paul never treated different groups of people in the same way when he preached the gospel. He did not have a common approach that he imposed on everybody. Look at the contrast between two of his messages. In Acts 13:16-41 when he preaches in a synagogue in Pisidian Antioch his point of contact is their history and his point of conflict is the Law (13:39). But in Acts 14:15-17 in his spontaneous 'preach' to the crowd in Lystra which is about to sacrifice to him and Barnabas, Paul never mentions the Jewish Scriptures. Instead his point of contact is creation and his point of conflict is idolatry.

---

1. Timothy Keller, *Center Church* (Grand Rapids: Zondervan, 2012), p. 48.

Whenever we're communicating the gospel there needs to be both of these aspects in play: contact and conflict. We need to connect with the cultural or sub-cultural narratives. But at some point we also need to demonstrate how the gospel story conflicts with that narrative. This is the sharp end of the gospel. This is where the call to repentance is focused.

We must not fear culture, nor should we be indifferent to it either. One problem of the Western world, and particularly the English-speaking Western world, is the assumption that 'pop culture' is universal and defining. But that can mask significant differences between local contexts. Just because someone in Tehran might understand some cultural references, drink Coca-Cola, listen to hip-hop or know who Johnny Depp is, does not mean we're culturally connected. Many Americans, for example, undergo serious culture shock when they move to the U.K. because they have failed to appreciate the cultural differences between America and Britain. It doesn't take long to get through the veneer of pop culture and hit the hard rock of what we might call 'deep' culture.

It's impossible to be context neutral. Paul was culturally savvy. He was a Jew for sure, a 'Hebrew of Hebrews'. But he was also from Tarsus, which was 'no mean city' (Acts 21:39). It was a centre of learning and a place of high culture that rivalled both Athens and Rome. So Paul was not raised in some isolated cultural enclave. And this showed in his ability to adapt for the sake of the gospel. The key to planting in any context is to be contextual, so that when we share the gospel we can show how the light of the gospel illuminates the surrounding culture, both celebrating its achievements and exposing its flaws.

3. Have a passion for people

We see Paul's passion for people very clearly in his time in Athens in Acts 17. It seems Paul never intended to stay in the city or gather a gospel community. It was a stop-over as he waited for Silas and Timothy, having just been escorted out of Berea by a group of concerned disciples. But once there, he cannot help himself. He is profoundly impacted by what he sees. The city is straining under the weight of idolatry, and he is profoundly jealous for God's glory. He sees ignorance and sin, and his heart breaks.

Planting churches is not a sociological exercise where we do our research by reading the books, visiting the local shops and talking to local people. It is not about questionnaires and data analysis. Of course, all of these can be helpful. But church planting is essentially about loving people and being moved by the glory of God.

In Mark 6:34 when Jesus saw a large crowd 'he had compassion on them'. The word Mark uses shows that it was a deep-rooted affective response to their plight. You have to love the people among whom you are planting. You have to have a sense that these are *your* people. You must share their pain as well as their joys. There should be a sense that you would rather be here than anywhere else. If that is absent then pray for it. If you still fail to experience it, it probably means you're not out there in the community, shoulder-to-shoulder, eyeball-to-eyeball. You're not in the lives of the people, sharing their stories and carrying their burdens.

4. Start with shared connections

Paul had a predictable, but flexible, approach. He first visited the synagogue and then spent time with the God-fearers, those Gentiles who were attracted by the ethical monotheism of Judaism (Acts 14:1). Jews were culturally and theologically distant from most of the other inhabitants of pagan towns. But the God-fearers provided a cultural bridge for Paul: they were *theologically* connected to the Jews while also being *culturally* connected to the dominant culture of the city. So these were the people with whom Paul usually planted churches. They were providentially placed to be an effective bridgehead. In other words, there was a strategic importance of God-fearers.

In the early days of planting, we face the temptation of doing everything and being spread too thinly. Yet no one can reach everyone. So it is better to reach the people you can reach. Reach those with whom you establish some kind of connection whether that be through a shared culture, dispositions or interests. It may be that, initially, we need to be content to see something homogenous develop. We can and should then call maturing believers to embrace diversity in Christ and train them to become all things to all men for the sake of the gospel. But in the initial stages be happy to be opportunistic for the sake of the gospel. Work hard by all means, but also work smart.

5. Build community

The term 'church' is the usual translation of the Greek word *ekklesia* which means 'gathering'. So some argue that 'church' only exists in the event of gathering. But in Acts 9:31 Luke talks about 'the church throughout all Judea and Galilee and Samaria'. The term 'church' in the singular is used to refer to what would have been multiple 'churches' throughout a region of around 5,000 square miles. So, as David Peterson[2] argues, it seems the New Testament uses *ekklesia* in a more developed sense. It refers to *those the Lord has gathered to Himself* and not merely to the *act of gathering at a specific moment*. In this 'virtual world', it is important to emphasise that I am not relegating the physical act of gathering together as church to a mere preference or in some way incidental. A church to be a local church needs to gather. What I am arguing for is simply that the act of meeting together once a week is not the sum total of what it means to be the church in a locale. For example, it doesn't seem Paul is simply talking about an act of gathering when writing to Timothy about the appointment of elders. The apostle draws a direct line between the day-to-day managing of a household and taking care of the church of God (1 Tim. 3:5). I suspect Paul has more in mind than hymns, notices and crowd control when he talks of taking care of the church of God. A few verses later he says: 'I am writing these things to you so that, if I delay, you may know how one ought to behave in the household of God, which is the church of the living God, a pillar and buttress of truth' (1 Tim. 3:14-15). The family household has a corporate identity and relationship beyond the times when they are together in the house. In the same way the church ('the household of God') has an identity

2. David Peterson, 'The Locus of the Church – Heaven or Earth' (6 October 2016), The Theologian, <http://www.theologian.org.uk/ church/locus.html>

and relationship beyond the times when we are physically meeting together. The act of gathering is one expression (a very important expression) of what it means to be the community of Christ. But there is more to church than Sunday mornings. Christ has called his people to meet together, formally and informally, and share our lives together under the authority of His word.

This is important because what we understand by church is going to shape our approach to church planting. If we think church is simply about the Sunday meeting then the majority of our effort will go into that event. We might even be tempted to think that once that event is up and running then our job is done. But going public with a meeting is easy. The hard work of church planting is building a community of disciples through the Holy Spirit.

Church planting is about seeing an authentic and alternative community created through the gospel by the Spirit, a community which models the reign of Christ and invites others into that community through the gospel.

6. Appoint and train leaders

Paul and Barnabas preach the gospel on the way out during their first missionary journey and then appoint elders on their way back (Acts 14:21-23). In a similar way, Titus is left in Crete to appoint elders everywhere on the island where there was now a church (Titus 1:5).

Godly leadership is vital for the well-being of the church. So church planters should get on with appointing leaders as soon as is feasible and wise. Some church planters are reluctant to do this, and there are numerous reasons for this hesitancy, but do it we must. The church we plant under God is not our plaything, nor our own little fiefdom that we rule. It is God's church, and God will provide leaders who meet the criteria of 1 Timothy 3 and Titus 1. Our task as planters is to recognise them. The characteristics of eldership taught by Paul in 1 Timothy 3 reflect an ordinary, street-level godliness which is revealed in the context of everyday life. Perhaps the reason Paul and Barnabas could appoint leaders so swiftly is because they looked for men in whom there was evidence of common grace. They weren't impressed by superficial ability; what mattered was solid character proved over a period of time.

The task of the church planter is to get such leaders in place, equipped as theologians-in-residence. This allows the planter to move on to plant again. It can be an error for a church planter to get drawn into providing on-going pastoral oversight in a church when he has the gifting and temperament to plant multiple congregations.

Conclusion

One of the joys of a preacher is the opportunity to rehearse the gospel time after time. One of the joys of a writer is to be reminded, in the act of writing, of the topic in hand. As I have rehearsed these truths and journeyed with Luke, I have been encouraged afresh in the task of church planting to which we are all, in some shape or form, called. We live in a fast-changing world. Yet we cannot doubt the sovereignty of God in history and human affairs. Neither can we doubt his goodness, providence or wisdom in placing us right here, right now.

This is a time of gospel opportunity. The challenge before us is to grasp this opportunity with thankful hands and hearts. Church planting is one of the primary ways for us to do this. It gives us the opportunity to think at a fundamental level about what it means to be the people of God and how we make the good news of Jesus known to this generation. In this sense, our task is no different to that of any other generation. We know that other generations responded obediently and bore fruit for God's glory, even during times of great hardship and spiritual apostasy. Our task is not new, but it is urgent.

This is how we articulate it in the final one of our five doctrinal distinctives of Acts 29:

> We embrace a missionary understanding of the local church and its role as the primary means by which God chooses to establish his kingdom on earth. The church has a clear biblical mandate to look beyond its own community to the neighbourhood, the nation, and the world as a whole; thus mission is not an optional program in the church but an essential element in the identity of the church. We are called to make Christ known through the gospel and, by the power of the Holy Spirit, to bring his lordship to bear on every dimension of life. The primary way we fulfil this mission is through the planting of churches that plant churches and the training of their leaders. Our aim is that Jesus Christ would be more fully formed in each person through the ministry of those churches God enables us to plant around the world. We also believe we are responsible neither to retreat from our culture nor to conform to it, but with humility, through the Spirit and the truth of the gospel, to engage it boldly as we seek its transformation and submission to the lordship of Christ.

Christian Focus Publications

Our mission statement –

STAYING FAITHFUL

In dependence upon God we seek to impact the world through literature faithful to His infallible Word, the Bible. Our aim is to ensure that the Lord Jesus Christ is presented as the only hope to obtain forgiveness of sin, live a useful life and look forward to heaven with Him.

Our Books are published in four imprints:

CHRISTIAN FOCUS

popular works including biographies, commentaries, basic doctrine and Christian living.

CHRISTIAN HERITAGE

books representing some of the best material from the rich heritage of the church.

MENTOR

books written at a level suitable for Bible College and seminary students, pastors, and other serious readers. The imprint includes commentaries, doctrinal studies, examination of current issues and church history.

CF4•K

children's books for quality Bible teaching and for all age groups: Sunday school curriculum, puzzle and activity books; personal and family devotional titles, biographies and inspirational stories – because you are never too young to know Jesus!

Christian Focus Publications Ltd,
Geanies House, Fearn, Ross-shire,
IV20 1TW, Scotland, United Kingdom.
www.christianfocus.com